To Alex

Something rediscover'd -

, cool

V.C.

Blackships
and
Thanadelthur

by Rick Book

With illustrations by
Amanda Dow

Featuring photography by
Dennis Fast, Manitoba
Francis Lépine, Quebec

Series editor
Barbara Huck

Heartland

Heartland Publications
Winnipeg, Canada

Printed in Manitoba, Canada

Credits

Audio reading
Nicola St. John

Graphic design, layout & maps
Dawn Huck

Icon illustrations
Shereen Ramprashad

Research assistance
Jane Huck

Prepress
ImageColor 2000, Winnipeg, Canada

Printing
Printcrafters, Winnipeg, Canada

National Library of Canada Cataloguing in Publication Data

Book, Rick
Blackships & Thanadelthur
(Young heroes of North America ; v. 1)
Includes bibliographical references.
ISBN 1–896150–12–8 (with CD) — ISBN 1–896150–13–6 (without CD)

1. Domagaya, fl. 1534- —Juvenile fiction.
2. Taignoagny, fl. 1534- —Juvenile fiction.
3. Thanadelthur, d. 1717—Juvenile fiction. I. Dow, Amanda. II. Title.
III. Series: Book, Rick. Young heroes of North America ; v. 1.
PS8553.O636B52 2001   jC813'.54   C2001-910661-0   PZ7.B6456B1 2001

Heartland Associates Inc.
PO Box 103, RPO Corydon
Winnipeg, MB R3M 3S7
www.hrtlandbooks.com
5 4 3 2 1

Wildflowers bloom in late June along the coast of Hudson Bay, a stark contrast to the region's ancient blue granite. These rocks are among the oldest in the world.

Acknowledgements

Blackships

My sincere thanks to Dr. Jean-Pierre Chrestien, head of Historical Archaeology at the Museum of Civilization in Hull, Quebec, and Claude Paulette, historian and editor of *Le Monde de Jacques Cartier* in Ste-Foy, Quebec, for reading the manuscript, making corrections and offering their expert insights. I am also grateful to Angeline Dazé, Eileen Meillon and Guy Vadeboncoeur at The Stewart Museum at the Fort in Montreal for their kind assistance.

In France, I was assisted by Dr. Gilles Foucqueron, président de l'Association Malouine des Amis de Jacques Cartier in Saint-Malo, while Bernard Leman of Toronto and Suzanne Benoit of Toronto and Paris assisted with translation, research and, in the case of Suzanne, telephone interviews in French.

Rod Kitchen, hunter, professional meat-cutter and gun safety instructor in Orillia, Ontario, gave me advice on hunting; Joe and Judy Hanson of Montreal extended their hospitality as always and the staff of the Toronto Public Library in many locations, including the Metro Reference Library, were always courteous and helpful.

I am also grateful to the following readers for their generous comments and criticisms: Alison Book, Carolyn Beck, Anne Carter, Avril Dell, Ann Thomas, Greer Thomas, Richard Ungar, Werner Lichtenberger and Katya Verikaitus.

Thanadelthur

My sincere gratitude to Flora Beardy, Director of the Aboriginal Heritage Program at York Factory First Nation in York Landing, Manitoba; Gladys Powderhorn, council member and former chief of the Dene-Sayisi First Nation in Tadoule Lake, Manitoba; Lanette Huculak from Parks Canada in Churchill, Manitoba; Raymond Sonfrere, project coordinator of Elders Restoring Balance at the Dene Cultural Institute in Hay River, Northwest Territories, and Sylvia Van Kirk, professor of history at the University of Toronto, all of whom read the manuscript, made corrections and offered their expert insights.

Thanks also to Bob Coutts, Parks Canada historian in Winnipeg, for research material; Dennis Fast, wildlife and Arctic photographer from Kleefeld, Manitoba, for his wonderful photographs of northern lands; Shirley Irving for her research into Scottish and Orcadian speech, and the staff at the Toronto Public Library.

Finally, I am grateful to these readers who made very helpful comments: Alison Book, Pierce Desrochers-O'Sullivan, Darcie Dixon, Wendy Dixon, Hadley Dyer, Joe Hanson, Nancy Harvey, Kym Kean, Doug Macfarlane, Alexander Offord, Sarah Reynolds, Samantha Souccar, Audrey Souccar, Maggie Wygant and Katya Verikaitis.

Contents

Coming home: Domagaya and Taignoagny spot familiar shores.

Blackships

Maybe when we get back Cartier and his French will have left for home, Taignoagny thought. But there was something gnawing in his gut, something bad.

PART ONE
July 1534
Somewhere near Baie de Gaspé

Sunlight glinted off the knife-sharp edge, its stone point quivering slightly as Domagaya pulled back the string. His right eye aimed past the feather, down the wooden shaft. Stillness. The forest held its breath. The woodland caribou raised his antlered head. Sniffed.

Thwrung!

The arrow shot past the trembling aspen, between the mottled, unravelling birch, pierced the shiny, tawny coat behind the buck's left shoulder, carved through thin muscle, grazed a rib and sliced into its heart in midbeat. The caribou dropped to its knees, lowered its head into a slanting shaft of light, and with a final sigh fell on its side into the bed of lichen it had been eating.

"Good shot." Taignoagny smiled. But his older brother was already running, leaping over a deadfall, toward his prize.

"Wahay," his voice rang through the woods, the timeless cry of a young hunter exulting in his kill. Taignoagny ran to catch up, stopped beside Domagaya as he stood by his buck, knife drawn, head raised.

"Thank you, Cudouagny, for this gift that you have given your people." Then he leaned over, lifted the buck's head by the antlers and, with one smooth stroke, slit its neck.

"Yaeii!" Domagaya dropped the buck's head as Taignoagny screamed. The two boys stared at its neck, at the liquid bubbling out of the knife cut. Thick, oozing liquid, not red, but black. Fear gripped the boys like winter. The animal slowly raised its head and looked at them; storm clouds roiled

Domagaya
the elder son of Donnacona, an Iroquois leader

Taignoagny
the second son of Donnacona

Cudouagny
the name of the Iroquois God, according to Jacques Cartier's journals

3

across its eyes. The cut in its neck began to move, like a mouth speaking, but no words came.

Domagaya stumbled backward, fell into a juniper bush and scrambled to his feet. "Run!" he yelled but Taignoagny needed no command. The two turned and ran, breechcloths flapping, moccasins flying, branches flailing as they passed. They ran blindly, wildly, anywhere at first, then finally angled back to their father's camp. He was agouhanna, the village leader. He would know what this meant.

Donnacona nodded his head slightly. His two sons stood before him in the dim bark hut. Now, at his signal, they sat to one side, cross-legged on the dirt floor. A thin ribbon of smoke from a small fire rose toward a hole in the roof. Errant wisps curled across the pole and bark roof and cast a fine grey blanket over the sachem, shamans and elders gathered there. They had smoked their pipes, then listened to the story of young Domagaya's kill, of the black blood and of the wound that spoke without words.

"This is a sign, to be sure," said Agona, the fierce battle-scarred sachem of the Turtle clan. "Remember the Toudamans who massacred our people last summer on their journey here. This sign means trouble for us." A murmur of agreement. Domagaya looked at his brother, clearly excited to be part of this fearsome mystery.

"We have come a long way from our village to fish and to look for the pale visitors who come in wind canoes." It was Contarea, the brothers' uncle, shaman of their grandmother's clan. The carved bones that hung from his ears shook and rattled as he spoke. On the end of his magic stick, the skull of an eagle screamed without sound. "I, too, believe this is an omen. There will be danger ahead. We must prepare to face it bravely."

Carhagouha, matron of the Snipe clan, rose. "My counsel is for caution," she said. "I have a bad feeling about this business. Perhaps it means we should return home to Stadacona." A low grumbling rumbled through the assembly. Taignoagny looked at Domagaya in surprise.

agouhanna
the principal civic leader of an Iroquoian province or region

Donnacona
the principal leader of Kanata, the Iroquois province or region surrounding what is now Quebec City

sachem
(SA-kem) a chief or high ranking official. The term is also used in a number of Algonquian-speaking cultures; it comes from the early Algonquian *saakimaawa* or chief

4

It was not like the Snipe clan to run from danger. Carhagouha let the voices die down before she continued. "Maybe we should let the Mi'kmaq trade with these strangers who are so powerful. And we will trade with the Mi'kmaq from the safety of our community, as we have done in the past." Another murmur. Domagaya sensed more disagreement with Carhagouha's words.

"Teandewiata, you have not spoken," Donnacona called to the darkest corner of the hut. An old man stirred. Two younger men helped the bent, withered war sachem to his feet. A tattered wolf pelt was draped around his shoulders, the grinning head hung across his bony chest. Teandewiata's long white hair and crooked nose gave him a fierce look, which was undone by the twinkle in his eye. He was one of the boys' favourites.

"This summer I could have stayed in Stadacona to tell stories and scare birds away from the corn." His words fell as softly as leaves. Domagaya and Taignoagny leaned forward. There was silence in the council. "Yet I have come here. I have lived more than sixty summers. I have been in many great battles and seen many great things. Many things ... " His voice trailed off as his mind journeyed over the days of his life.

"But!" he shouted suddenly, as if gaining strength from the words welling up inside him. "I have heard the stories about these strange men, of their wind canoes that come across the great sea from lands far, far away. I confess that I am curious. I want to see these pale creatures, for they have powers we do not have. We may learn from them and make better lives for our children and their children. Perhaps we can make a treaty with them that will bring us wealth, or weapons that will protect us from our enemies. Friends, we must not be afraid of the days yet to come for we might as well run from the rising sun. We are warriors. We are Iroquois. That is all I have to say."

A week passed. Life in the camp had returned to normal. Far out on the wide bay, a northeast wind blew, bringing fog and a cold misting rain. Deep in the sheltered narrow end of the bay near their camp, women with reed baskets dug clams on the tidal flats; others strung nets of hemp between poles to catch mackerel when the tide came in. Hunting parties searched the dripping forest for game. A short path led away from the beach into the forest. There, the tribe's summer huts stood in a grassy clearing by a river that flowed into the bay. Outside the huts, women sat by their fires and talked while strips of boar, porcupine and deer slowly smoked. Inside one, Teandewiata, the oldest sachem, napped fitfully on his sleeping skins. It was a brooding, dull day; even the crows were silent.

shaman
(SHAW-men or SHAY-men) a priest of shamanism, or medicine man among many native North American cultures. The religious practice of shamanism rested on the belief that good and evil spirits pervade the world and could be summoned through people with special powers. The word dates back to Sanskrit, the oldest known member of Indo-European languages.

Stadacona
the Iroquois village in Kanata where Donnacona's people resided when Europeans first arrived in 1534. The village was located where Old Quebec City now lies.

Mi' kmaq
(MIG-maw) an Algonquian-speaking people who were living along the Gulf of St. Lawrence in the early 1500s

mackerel
(MAK-er-el) a fish found along the Atlantic coast

Protected coves, like this one, were ideal for summer fishing camps. People fished for mackerel and hunted along the shores of the great river.

Domagaya and Taignoagny walked along a wooded path that ran parallel to the shore. They'd been on lookout duty all night on the point of land that protected their bay from the roaring wind and waves. Two friends had just replaced them. They'd joked about who'd won and lost at gambling the night before, then the brothers headed home to sleep. There were other guards across the bay, all keeping watch for enemy war parties or the pale strangers. After much discussion in the council, it was agreed that the tribe would meet with the strangers if they came. Donnacona had ordered extra lookouts posted.

"I don't know about you, brother, but I am afraid of these people," Taignoagny confided. "I hope we don't see them."

Domagaya scowled. This was his fifteenth summer. He was tall and sinewy, strong like his father, his head shaved except for the knot of black hair on top tied with a leather cord as was the custom. He had intense brown

Hayahhh!

eyes, carried himself erect and was proud of the scars he bore from the rites of passage. He had not cried out. He looked at his younger brother sharply. "You speak like a Toudamans."

Taignoagny winced. He was only thirteen and had not yet entered manhood, so his hair was uncut and hung to his shoulders. He had rounder features, like his mother they said. He had never known her. In spite of the skill of the midwife, in spite of the magic of Contarea's potions and the healers' chants, she had died a week after giving birth to him. A painful death, yet she had made no sound. He had been raised by Contarea's wife, Estahagao, and by their grandmother, Sadeguenda, matron of the Bear clan.

"Hayahhhh!" The yell came from behind them. Someone was running through the bush toward them. The brothers turned, lowered their spears and crouched, ready to fight. But it was Touaguiainchain, one of the lookouts, who burst out of the trees.

"They're here!" He stopped in front of them, gasping, his unstrung bow and spear in his hand. "Black wind canoes. Two big ones. And a smaller one paddling near shore. Alert the camp!" Without waiting for a reply, Touaguiainchain wheeled and raced back, his buckskin quiver of arrows dancing on his brown back as he disappeared into the bush.

Taignoagny, face still burning with shame at his cowardice, at the sting of his brother's words, raced down the path. He was shorter, with a square sturdy body but strong legs. He would show Domagaya. He would outrun him and be first to deliver the news.

But the camp already knew; the drums had started, calling everyone back. As Taignoagny ran out of the forest, people scrambled everywhere. Women gathered the children and the food. They would hide in the forest, guarded by a group of young men. A hunting party ran out on the far side of the clearing, a boar swinging wildly on a pole between two men. They threw it on the ground and ran to the huts to get ready. For what, no one was sure. No one knew what the strangers would bring. The boar could wait.

"Let's get our war paint on," said Domagaya who'd caught up to him. The two boys arrived at their bark house just as their father came out. Donnacona had on his beaver headdress with its shining abalone shells, snake rattles, and an eagle feather. His face was painted red with marks of black and yellow around his eyes. Over his shoulders hung the great bear robe that marked him agouhanna. A necklace of bear teeth and claws looped across

quiver
a portable case for arrows, from the Norman French quevier

abalone
(AB-e-lon-ey) a large marine mollusk with an ear-shaped shell. The interior of the shell had a colourful, pearly finish that was used by many cultures for making ornaments.

his chest. Taignoagny's heart filled with courage at the sight.

"Hurry," Donnacona said.

"Wait! Father!" A boy, almost six, broke away from his mother as their group headed into the forest. It was Miscou, the son of Donnacona's Mi'kmaq wife, Neguac, whom he had purchased three years ago. Donnacona looked across the field at her, saw her worried look, but took the boy's hand anyway and strode with him to the beach.

ochre
(O-ker)
a naturally occurring red, yellow or brown mineral oxide of iron, usually found mixed with clay or sand. Ochre was used as paint by many cultures.

Inside the hut, Contarea, a wolf head and pelt draped over his head and back, danced and sang as a circle of shamans pounded drums and chanted. It was a song to the great spirit, Cudouagny, asking for courage, praying for victory over their enemies. Taignoagny and Domagaya raced to the place along the wall where they slept, grabbed more arrows and jammed them into their quivers. They ran to the gourds where the war paint – red ochre mixed with clay – was kept. They plunged their hands in, hearts pounding as they smeared their faces.

Haiiii!   "Haiiii!" A cry came from outside. The drumming stopped. The brothers ran out to see, with Contarea and the shamans behind them. On the beach, Donnacona and a large group of warriors looked out to the bay, at a low black shape on the water.

A canoe.

It had rounded the point where Domagaya and Taignoagny had spent the night and was making its way along the shore. But these strangers were not paddling. It was something else. Long thin sticks stuck out from each side of the wide canoe. The sticks dipped into the water together, then came out. The movement was repeated again and again.

Like a poisonous beetle clawing its way toward us, Taignoagny thought. He swallowed, grabbing his knife instinctively. Black blood on the forest floor.

Everyone was on the beach. The warriors bristled with spears. Bows were strung, arrows in hand. Taignoagny looked around. Hidden

Ohhhhhh

in the trees, more warriors watched, ready for a surprise attack. They could see heads in the canoe. Taignoagny counted eight, maybe nine.

"Ohhhhhh." A murmur rose from the Iroquois as a man stood up in the middle of the canoe. A man with a flat headdress.

"It's their sachem," someone said.

Taignoagny's heart banged against his chest like an otter in a trap. The canoe stopped, still far out in the bay. The long sticks lay still in the water. He could see pale-skinned men, some with headdresses, some bare-headed.

"What are they doing?"

"They're preparing their weapons."

Short sticks appeared, black ones that glinted in the sun. Thundersticks, the Mi'kmaq called them. Powerful, awful things that spoke with thunder and smoke. They fired not arrows, but balls of metal that tore men's heads off. The canoe rose and fell in the waves. The wind was dying. The air was heavy, wet, a wolf waiting to pounce. *Aaii! We are dead!*

"Look! Over there!" someone shouted.

"Aaii. We are dead!" another cried.

"Quiet!" Donnacona commanded.

Out on the bay beyond the point, a huge dark object appeared. In all his thinking about this day, Taignoagny had never imagined such a thing. It was more than a wind canoe. It was an island. A huge black island of wood drifting into the bay.

It rose to a sharp point at one end, like a canoe only much higher, with a long tree sticking out in front. The other end stood high into the air, like a longhouse. Above the canoe hung great clouds of animal skins of many shapes and sizes; all bellied out by the wind. They were held up by two tall trees; their branches cut off, with poles tied across them. Great spider webs of cords were attached to the trees and to the skins.

"Look! Another one!" someone shouted as a second wind canoe ghosted out from behind the peninsula.

"They must be from the spirit world," whispered Domagaya, "to build such canoes."

"What powers do these creatures have that they can make these things?"

"The white skins must be from giant animals. How do they kill such beasts?"

Donnacona had been silent. Now he held up his hand. The warriors and shamans stopped talking. "There is much magic here," he began. "But we have our own powerful magic and the Great Spirit to protect us. Let us

welcome these strangers as our guests." The strangers' smaller canoe started moving again.

"Launch the canoes," Donnacona said. "We will invite them to our camp."

In an instant, the salt water in the bay boiled as a hundred paddles churned the birch canoes toward the strangers. Domagaya and Taignoagny knelt in the middle of their father's canoe with Miscou and Contarea at the front. In no time, they were within a spear throw of the strangers' canoe. They stopped. Donnacona rose to his feet. The pale sachem stood up, too.

"Haiii" Donnacona called, raising his arm in the traditional way. "Welcome to Hongueda, the land of our people."

The visitor lifted his arm in a similar way and spoke. His words tumbled from his mouth. Like pebbles in a stream, Taignoagny thought. The stranger pointed to the great sea and then to his big wind canoes. The canoes had stopped. From across the distance, they heard a deep and chilling rattle. Something splashed into the water beside one canoe, then the other. Men hung in the air from the poles. The big white skins disappeared as the Iroquois watched. The stranger stopped talking.

These men have hair growing out of their faces, Taignoagny thought and looked to see if they had claws. They didn't.

It was Donnacona's turn to speak. "We are the people of Kanata on the great river. We journey here every summer to fish and hunt. Come to our camp." He pointed to the shore. "Feast with us and we will talk of friendship and trade."

Their animal skins are so fine, wondered Taignoagny. What amazing creatures they must have in their lands.

Donnacona pointed again to the shore. "Come. We have fresh meat and fish. You are our guests and you must eat." He picked up his paddle, turned their canoe and headed for shore. According to plan, the cooking fires were already burning. The elder women had watched from the trees while they butchered the boar. Now they turned the pieces slowly on cords over the fires as the flotilla of Iroquois canoes formed an escort to shore.

As the nose of the visitors' heavy canoe grated on the sand, the pale sachem rose and smiled. His hair under his headdress was short, not long. No bear grease. Most important of all – no war paint. Brown curly hair covered his face from his sharp nose to his sharp chin. Like a weasel, thought Taignoagny.

The stranger jumped onto the beach. He had a black hide around his

Hongueda
the region of Gaspé

Kanata
the region along the St. Lawrence around what is now Quebec City, which gave its name to Canada

waist which held a very long knife with a carved and shiny metal handle. But before he approached the waiting Donnacona, the man went down on one knee, looked up at the sky, and made a sign.

"He's praying," Domagaya whispered.

The stranger rose and walked up to Donnacona, who towered over him. He took off his hat, swept it down as he bent slightly toward the Iroquois leader. "Cartier," he said in his strange tongue. "Captain Jacques Cartier, sailing from the port of Saint-Malo on the coast of France for His Majesty, King François 1st." Not one word was understood, except perhaps that the stranger's name sounded like Kart-yeh. For some reason it made Taignoagny think of the caribou wound, talking without words.

For the first time, the Iroquois chief smiled. "Donnacona," he responded. "Donnacona. I am agouhanna of Kanata." The pale Kart-yeh, smiled, nodded. Donnacona pointed out the clan sachems and shamans, then Domagaya, Taignoagny and Miscou. He said their names, then pointed at himself. Again the pale sachem nodded and smiled.

Donnacona swept his arms wide and explained again that the Iroquois were living here for the summer, that their permanent home was several day's paddle from here. He said they had come to fish and to see the strangers, that they would like to make peace with them and learn the magic of their ways.

Cartier nodded politely, also without understanding a word. He turned to his men, waved them forward. Together, with their thundersticks in their arms, they walked to the fires, nodding to the old women cooking. A woman carved off a choice piece, offered it to the visiting leader, but he shook his head. They inspected the canoes. Cartier ran his hands across the bark, the pitch seams and the spruce root cords tying the bark to the gunwales. "Where do you sleep?" He asked in his tongue.

Donnacona nodded, pointing to the canoes. "Yes, we travelled here in these. It took five days for our journey."

Cartier again nodded, then quickly turned and led his men back to their canoe.

They're leaving already! Taignoagny was astounded.

As his men pushed the canoe into the water and jumped in, Cartier motioned for Donnacona to follow. Mystified by the visitors' strange behavior, the Iroquois again got in their canoes, and followed them out to the ships.

The wind canoes were fearsome things. As they got closer, the black walls rose high into the air. Like the cliffs at Stadacona, thought Taignoagny, heart beating, his mouth as dry as a toad.

The poles of the canoe towered above them like dead pines on a mountain ridge. The white skins were now rolled and tied. There were cords everywhere, huge and black. Some passed through pieces of wood, some were tied like ladders that reached to the top of the poles. Others hung in tangled clumps. The wind canoe reeked, a pungent, bitter smell.

Donnacona signalled for the Iroquois to stop. They watched as Cartier climbed up the wall of the wind canoe on ladders made of cords. He turned and waved them closer.

Two of the strangers climbed down the ropes and got into their canoe as the Iroquois approached. They carried bags out of which they pulled shiny knives. They handed one each to Donnacona and Contarea. Donnacona smiled, feeling its sharpness with his thumb. To the boys, the strangers gave strings of beautiful coloured stones. As each canoe came up, the wondrous gifts were handed out and the Iroquois paddled off to make room while they admired these treasures. Some people stood and sang songs of thanks to the pale strangers.

That night, as each family gathered around the cooking fires, they talked of all that they had seen this day and marvelled at the beauty of their gifts.

The next morning, the wind canoes were still there, black and quiet. The Iroquois watched from shore as the strangers moved around on them. From time to time, they heard whistles and shouts across the water. In the afternoon, a cry went up on shore. The strangers were coming again, this time in two canoes.

Again Cartier stepped ashore and greeted Donnacona with a friendly smile. Then he called to one of his men who came forward with a blanket and a small sack. He knelt on the beach, rolled the blue blanket out on the sand, then began pulling objects out of the sack, placing them carefully on the blanket.

Domagaya stared. It was as if the man had reached to the sky, pulled down the stars and laid them at the feet of his people. They shone like sunlight glancing off the water, like rocks sparkling after a rain. The warriors, sachem, shamans and the three women who had stayed behind crowded forward to look.

Cartier kneeled and picked up a large, round shiny object. It had a yellow stone in the middle, gleaming like a lynx eye in firelight. He rose before

Donnacona and unfastened a small metal needle on the back, as slender as a porcupine's quill. He put it against Donnacona's bear robe, pushed the needle in, then backed away. The metal with the yellow stone shone. Donnacona smiled, nodded to Cartier. He turned to show off his gift. "Perhaps this is the eye of the Great Spirit," he said.

Donnacona signalled to a warrior. He stepped forward with a new bow, a quiver of new arrows, and a silver-grey wolf pelt. Donnacona handed them to Cartier carefully. "These are gifts from my people," he said. Cartier nodded, examined the bow and the feathered arrows, then ran his hand through the long fur of the wolf pelt. He seemed pleased and said something to Donnacona. It was only then that Taignoagny realized he'd been holding his breath. Domagaya heard him exhale, turned and cracked a tiny smile.

The feast went well. The Iroquois danced and sang songs of great legends for the strangers as they sat on the grass near the beach. The women served steaming chunks of boar and venison and a mash of corn and squash and beans on pieces of bark. The visitors did not bring spoons, but they drew their knives and cut the meat and even ate the mash from the tips of their weapons. The trading had been a success, too. The Iroquois wore shining necklaces, strings of coloured beads, brooches, earrings, metal knives, bracelets, coloured ribbons, even the blue trading blanket, which went to old Teandewiata.

Cartier had given each of the three women a comb and little metal pieces that sang like a bird when they were shaken. At this, the other women hiding in the woods were brought out and they received gifts as well. Then the strangers got into their canoe and went back to their wind canoes, resting like black ducks in the bay.

The next morning, two of the visitors' small canoes headed for the shore. Donnacona was summoned by the lookouts. "They are not coming here," he said to Angoutenc, who stood beside him, new red ribbons tied in his hair.

"What are those devils up to?" Angoutenc replied. His wife was no longer impressed with her new metal ring and singing metal. She would have preferred a sharp new knife.

"We've been tricked," she'd said.

The canoes with stick paddles headed for a point of land that interrupted the long sweep of the bay. The excited talk of the Iroquois grew quieter with

We've been tricked.

This sweep of beach and shore looks out on what is now called the Strait of Jacques Cartier.

every stroke. They watched the canoes touch shore and the men get out. They carried a long white pole with the bark scraped off.

The Iroquois watched as the strangers dug a hole. They could see Cartier standing watching, talking with his men. Then the strangers raised the pole into the air, slid one end into the hole and tilted the other end until it stood up straight.

"Look! There's a second pole across the big one." It was Carhagouha. Taignoagny remembered how she had spoken out in council against meeting with the strangers.

"Why are they doing that on our land?" someone asked.

"I saw the same shapes hanging from their necks," said a warrior.

"Is it a god? See, they are praying to the pole." The visitors had dropped to their knees. They faced the pole, heads bare and bowed. Then the strangers got into their canoes and paddled back to their wind canoes.

"Something bad is happening," Domagaya whispered to his brother. "I think these strange men will bring us trouble."

Donnacona motioned to some of the war sachem. "Come. I want to see this thing." Once again, Domagaya, Taignoagny and Miscou jumped into the canoe with their uncle and father. It would be the last footprint the two brothers would leave on their land for more than a year.

The stranger's pole was as high as five tall men. The white, smooth wood had been made square. Near the top, another white pole stretched across it. Like a man opening his arms to the sea, Taignoagny thought. Beneath the crosspole, there was a shiny metal shield with three wooden pieces like flowers attached to it, and above it, a piece of wood with markings carved deeply into it.

"What do you think the marks say?" Donnacona asked Contarea.

"I don't know," the shaman answered. "It could be a message to their creator."

"What if they have done this to claim our land?" asked Donnacona. "Perhaps they want it for themselves."

"If that is so, these men are evil," said Angoutenc. "Surely they would not do such a thing."

Especially after the feast we gave them, thought Taignoagny.

Donnacona had made up his mind. "They must take it down." They paddled grimly, straight for the nearest wind canoe, the one to which Cartier had gone. As the birchbark canoes closed the distance, they could see the strangers running to watch. A few had thundersticks.

"Kart-yeh!" Donnacona called out to the faces looking down from the black wall. "I want to speak to Kart-yeh."

Cartier's head appeared at once, his smile quickly vanquished by the look on Donnacona's face.

"What is this thing you have put on our land?" Donnacona turned, pointed at the poles on shore, made a symbol of them by holding two fingers across each other. "You have no right to erect these poles and make your marks upon them." He swept his hand across the bay, gesturing from horizon to horizon. "This land is a gift from our Creator. It is entrusted to us. It is not your land."

He pointed to his chest, pretended to fire an arrow across the bay. "Our people and the Mi'kmaq people have hunted and fished here since the little creeks and mighty rivers began to run and the forests covered the hills and valleys with green." Donnacona paused, eyes flashing. He jabbed a finger at Cartier. "You have come for one visit, as strangers, and we welcomed you and exchanged gifts with you and feasted together as friends. All this we have done in the spirit of hospitality, as is our custom. Your mark there is an arrow in the hearts of my people. You must take it down, Kart-yeh. This is our land." Donnacona stopped, waiting for a reply.

Cartier nodded. He had listened solemnly. He bent his head as one of his men whispered to him. Cartier waved Donnacona toward the wind canoe, held up an axe, made signs that he wanted to trade. He waved them closer again. As he did this, one of the strangers climbed down the rope ladder. He, too, waved Donnacona closer. And when they came close, the stranger grabbed their canoe and would not let go. Two more strangers scrambled down the cords and grabbed it, too. Cartier motioned for the Iroquois to climb up.

The brothers, watching their father, saw his eyes widen at the thought. He hesitated, looking past them to Contarea, then to the other sachem in their canoes. "We will go up," he said finally.

Cartier's men helped each one as they scrambled to the top of the wall and jumped down to the floor. "It's as big as a longhouse!" Taignoagny whispered to Domagaya. Their eyes were huge as they looked around: the towering poles that seemed to touch the sky, the thick black cords that lay everywhere, the many colours of clothing that the visitors wore. Domagaya ran his fingers across the wood. It was so smooth. There were no axe marks anywhere.

Cartier smiled. He held his arms in front of him, made two fingers cross each other like the poles on shore, then moved his head until the fingers were lined up with the poles. Then he pointed up to his ship and made a motion with his hand from his forehead out toward the landmark. He smiled at Donnacona, shrugged his shoulders, perhaps in frustration in their inability to speak each other's language.

"Contarea, what do you make of this?"

"I think he is saying that the mark is only a guide for their wind canoes."

"Do you believe him?"

"Perhaps."

longhouse
a long, rounded, wooden multi-family dwelling used mainly by Iroquoian-speaking peoples

17

The new clothes were made of strange materials.

Donnacona thought for a moment, turned to Cartier, pointed to the poles on shore, then gave him an abrupt and stern-faced nod.

Yes.

Cartier smiled with relief, called to his men and had them set up a table on the floor on the wind canoe. They brought out metal plates piled high with food. Perhaps the strangers aren't so rude after all, Taignoagny thought as they walked over to the table.

The strangers handed the Iroquois little cups of grey metal. A sour-looking man with a shaved head and weeping eye walked to each of them and poured out a light-coloured liquid, the colour of sap from the maple tree. Cartier spoke to Donnacona and his men. Then he held up his cup. His men all made similar motions, then they drank. The Iroquois watched them, then watched Donnacona who sniffed the container, held it up and drank.

Instantly, his eyes went wide; he slapped his chest and coughed, as the liquid burned its way down. The agouhanna paused for a moment, then smiled, nodded to his men. They all drank. *Ohheee*

"Ohheee." Taignoagny had never tasted anything so awful in his life. He wanted to spit it out, but he couldn't offend his hosts. Tears flooded his eyes, his chest felt on fire inside. He looked at Domagaya. His brother's face was full of pain, too.

Cartier waved the guests to the table, inviting them to eat. The boys put down the awful drinks and grabbed some meat. There were piles of cold auk, venison and salmon. The bread was darker in colour and much lighter in texture than the bannock the women in camp made. "This is good," Taignoagny said to Domagaya as he chewed.

Domagaya took another sip of the strangers' drink, shivered and smiled. "This fiery water is getting better."

The boys turned at the sound of laughter. One of the strangers had a small metal stick in his mouth. He blew it. Sounds came out like an eagle hunting, like the snow goose flying north in the spring. The song went faster and faster. Two strangers started dancing. The others laughed and clapped their hands. The Iroquois watched, holding out their cups as the man with the fiery drink came around again.

Cartier spoke to one of his younger men, who came to Domagaya and Taignoagny. Motioning for them to follow, he opened a wooden door that swung on its side. The stranger carried a small torch in a box. They followed him down a wooden ladder into the dark belly of the canoe. It was filled

auk
a black-and-white seabird of the north Atlantic coast. One of the largest species, the great auk, was hunted to extinction.

19

with strange shapes and shadows, as well as bitter smells. The man opened a large wooden box, pulled out some clothes and handed them to the boys.

"He is giving us these things," Domagaya said.

The Iroquois now realized that the strangers' clothes were not skins but were made of tiny threads as fine as the hair on cobs of corn. The man pointed again, motioned to the clothes.

"He wants us to put them on!" Doubt flashed through Taignoagny's mind. What will our father think? But Domagaya had already torn off his breech cloth. He stood naked in the dim light, holding one of the white shirts.

The young stranger nodded. He helped Domagaya slip the shirt over his head, poke his arms into the long sleeves. "I'm getting ready for winter," Domagaya joked. The stranger handed Domagaya some breeches. Domagaya stood on one leg, tried to slip them on and fell to the floor, laughing. "I wish this wind canoe would stand still." He laughed again.

In minutes, the brothers were fully dressed, including red pointed hats that flopped to one side on their heads. The young stranger pulled two metal necklaces out of the box and hung them around the boys' necks. They gleamed in the lamplight.

"You look like a stranger now," Taignoagny said with a grin.

"You look like the Trickster." Domagaya laughed. The visitor grinned and led them back up the wooden stairs.

As the boys walked out onto the deck of the ship, the music stopped. Donnacona turned and saw his sons. His mouth closed tightly, his eyes narrowed. Flashes of doubt flickered across his face. Then a loud laugh rang out. Contarea was pointing at them, howling. Donnacona glanced at his brother-in-law, then back to his sons. Finally, he allowed himself a small smile. It was all the brothers needed. They walked across to stand before him. The Iroquois gathered around, touching the clothes, admiring the texture and the colours.

Cartier spoke to Donnacona. He pointed to the two boys, to the ship, made signs of leaving, pointed to the sea beyond the point. He made signs

Trickster
in many native American cultures, a mythological creature with the ability to transform himself into many shapes, to play tricks on humans and teach them lessons. Some cultures believed the Trickster was a coyote.

20

of the ship sailing, then returning to this bay. At last, he pointed to the cross on shore.

Donnacona's face grew serious again. "He wants my sons to go with him."

Contarea said nothing.

Cartier smiled, pointed to his mouth, pointed to the boys, to their mouths, to his ears. "I think he wants them to teach him our tongue," Contarea said, not taking his eyes off Cartier.

"Perhaps he will teach them theirs," said Donnacona.

Domagaya and Taignoagny stood waiting. They had no choice in this decision. Domagaya's heart pounded like a war drum. He wanted to go, but also he didn't. Taignoagny knew exactly what he wanted – to go home to their village.

It was Contarea who sealed their fate. "Perhaps the boys can ride on the wind canoe as long as the strangers are visiting our land, to make sure they put up no more of their marks. Then they will return here when the strangers are ready to go back across the great sea."

Donnacona immediately saw the wisdom of the shaman's suggestion. He looked at his sons in their strange new clothes, then turned to Cartier and made signs. He pointed to the great sea, made the wind canoe motions that Cartier had made, made a circle of the lands nearby, then pointed to his sons and finally to himself. "My sons will ride on your canoe while you are visiting our lands," he said. "Then you must bring them back here before you return home."

Cartier nodded solemnly.

Donnacona turned to his sons. "You have an important task that will bring great honour among our people. Learn all you can from these visitors. Find out the true meaning of this mark and whether they put up any more. Learn their magic and their powerful secrets. Be brave, my sons."

Then he turned to Cartier. For the second time that day, he gave his assent with an abrupt nod.

Donnacona turned to his men. "We must go." They moved toward the ship's rail. Cartier spoke to him, held up the metal axe, pointed to the bear robe.

No! thought Taignoagny. He can't have my father's robe. Donnacona hesitated. His hand went to his robe, but his eyes went to the gleaming new axe in Cartier's hand. He undid the cord, removed his shiny eye gift and handed the great black pelt to the stranger. Then he took the axe and two new knives, glanced quickly at his sons, and climbed over the rail down to the canoes.

Sea stacks mark the coastline of the Mingan Archipelago on the north shore of the St. Lawrence. Today they are part of a national park.

The brothers ran to the rail, watched the Iroquois push away from the ship, turn and paddle to shore. They watched until the canoes were beached and their father, uncle and small brother disappeared into the forest. Until there was nothing left but fear and uncertainty.

The young man who had given them the clothes touched the brothers on the shoulders, motioning with his finger to follow. Reluctantly, they left the rail and walked toward the front of the ship. He showed them big round black metal things, like the hollow trunks of trees. And beside them, large metal balls.

Boom! "Boom!" said the young man, throwing his arms up.

The wind canoe was a busy place. Everywhere the pale strangers worked. Some pulled up water from the bay and washed the floor of the canoe with sticks and rags. Some tied strings around the ends of the big rough cords. One man had great folds of skins spread out on the deck and was patching a hole with a shiny metal needle. The young man with them pointed and talked, but finally gave up talking and just pointed at various things as he led them about the canoe.

Suddenly, there was a cry from one of the strangers. The boys looked up. A man standing in the cords above pointed to shore. Six birchbark canoes were headed toward them. The brothers ran to the rail. Has our father changed his mind? Is he coming to get us?

But as the canoes got closer, they could see that their father was not in them. Two of their aunts had come with Neguac and Miscou and some of their friends. They held up fresh fish and smoked meat wrapped in bark for the brothers. They handed them to the strangers who went down into their small canoe. Then the Iroquois waved at Cartier and pointing at the poles, told him they would not tear down his marks. When they left, the brothers felt something they had never known before – loneliness.

Later, as night approached, Cartier said something to the young man that caused his face to change, his smile to disappear. The man motioned to the boys to follow him, then led them down some dark steps. He stopped at a door and motioned for the boys to go in. It was a small room filled with great piles of skins like the ones they'd seen above. It had a strange smell like rotten mushrooms. The brothers went in, confused. The man motioned to a wooden bucket in the corner, pointing to his groin. Without smiling, without a word, he backed out of the room and closed the door. They heard metal jangling outside, then footsteps as he walked away. The white sliver of light at the bottom of the door flickered and disappeared. The brothers were in darkness.

Domagaya felt for the door. "We've been tricked! We're prisoners!" He pushed against the door hard, rattled the handle, but it was locked. "Why are they doing this?"

Taignoagny thought of his father removing his war sachem's robe, of his bare back as he returned to their camp without it, without them. "Why has our father let this happen?"

Quickly, they felt their way around the tiny room, wading through piles of fabric as deep as snowdrifts. There was no way out. Even the air seemed a prisoner, still and defeated. In shock, frightened that death might come at any moment, they sank down on the musty piles, but they could not sleep. Furry creatures ran over their legs and chewed noisily all night. It was too hot to sleep anyway. When will they come to kill us? Taignoagny wondered. I must be brave. I must die like an Iroquois.

In the morning, the boys heard noises above them: feet running, metal rattling, heavy thuds and creaks as the ship began to move. Only when they were well away, did the young man come and bring them up on deck. The boys ran to the rail and watched as the green coast of their summer camp grew smaller, until it became a thin black line on the horizon. We will never see our home again, Taignoagny thought. Without saying a word to each other, both thought of the dead buck in the forest. The omen had come true.

PART TWO
One year later, May 19, 1535
Saint-Malo, France

T he fleet had been blessed by White Robe, the Monseigneur of Saint-Malo; the captain and crew sprinkled with holy water. Then, after two days of waiting, the winds turned fair. The three ships spread their white wings and sailed for New France. That was what the French called it now since Cartier's one brief visit. A warm wind bellied out their sails, and the clanging iron bells of the stone cathedral grew faint as they sailed west toward the blue horizon. Neither Domagaya nor Taignoagny looked back at the walled port city, the way they had almost a year before when they'd left Hongueda.

"I cannot wait to see our father's face," said Domagaya as he coiled a line. Cartier had insisted that they work as sailors on the voyage home.

"It will take a winter's worth of fires to tell all we've seen," said Taignoagny as he pulled up a streaming bucket of seawater and used it to scrub the deck. Over the winter in France, he'd grown a hand taller, grown leaner, too. He'd also changed in other

ways. Where Domagaya had been eager to learn the tongue-twisting French and adapt to their strange ways, Taignoagny had resisted. There was a new look in his eyes, something hard.

Ten days out, bad weather struck. Thrashed by storms, the three ships became separated and lost sight of each other. For weeks, Cartier's *Grande Hermine* battled headwinds, rain and fog. Finally, after fifty tossing days at sea, a cry went up from the lookout on the mast: "Land ho!" It was Terra Nova. Cartier's expert navigation had brought them directly to this new found land.

The crew climbed into the rigging or ran to the rail. Domagaya still carried a medicine bag on a cord outside his French clothes. He retrieved some crumbled leaves of Saint-Malo corn, a substitute for tobacco, and sprinkled it over the side onto the hissing water as he offered up a prayer to the Creator. "Thank you, Cudouagny, for bringing us safely across the great sea." But there was a long way to go yet.

They sailed north and west to the island of Blanc Sablon off the northern tip of Terra Nova to await the other ships. When the weather-beaten *Petite Hermine* and *Emérillon* straggled in, they left to explore the unknown waters to the west. It was then that the brothers realized that Cartier had no intention of taking them directly to their father. Instead the three ships poked here and there, to that island, to this bay, crisscrossing the region, mapping the watery gateway to New France.

"We're searching for a passage to the Orient I told you about," Cartier explained one day. "We don't want to miss it." Over the winter, he'd spoken often of a strange land full of mysteries. Finding a shorter, safer route to the Orient was so important to the French that their king had paid for this entire expedition. "Do you know of such a passage?" Cartier had asked.

The brothers told him of the great river that flowed by Kanata. Its source was so far beyond Hochelaga, a large Iroquois community upstream, that no one had ever seen it. They noticed that Cartier's eyes shone every time they spoke of it. The king's had, too.

For the month of July, the three ships scoured the coasts and islands as they sailed westward. They anchored for a few days in St. Lawrence Bay, which Cartier had named a year ago after some dead French shaman. They were halfway through August before the brothers saw land they recognized.

"That is the island we saw after we left Hongueda," Domagaya told Cartier. The captain was surprised; he had not recognized it. Domagaya

Hochelaga (HOSH-e-la-ga) the Iroquoian province or region around what is now Montreal looked at the sun, then pointed south. "Our summer fishing camp is that way." Then he swung his arm west. "And the country of Saguenay is there, two days journey up the great river, and after that is Kanata." If the Frenchman heard the hopefulness in Domagaya's voice, he ignored it.

They sailed then along a southern coast and finding no passage, Cartier ordered the ships to steer north and east, back to St. Lawrence Bay. "Are we

Even upstream, where the St. Lawrence River narrows, fog often rolls in off the Atlantic, obscuring the low coastal mountains along the south shore.

never going to get home?" Taignoagny asked in exasperation as the crew swung the huge sails around. The ships then poked along a rocky northern coast with low, blue mountains sulking in the distance. Cartier paced the deck, his eyes constantly searching for an opening in the desolate shore that would signal he had found his precious passage.

One morning, they spied a huge watery gap in a deep cleft between two mountains. But to Cartier's disappointment it was the Saguenay River flowing swift and strong out of the north.

"Look!" Taignoagny pointed to the shore. "Canoes." His heart raced at this first sight of kindred people. There were four canoes. Two paddled toward the ships, but only one came near.

"Haii," called Domagaya. "I am Domagaya, son of Donnacona, agouhanna of Kanata." The four Saguenay men in the canoe talked excitedly. One called back.

"What are you doing on those creatures with wings? Are you from the spirit world?"

Domagaya paused. There was too much to explain. "No, my brother and I have been across the great water in these canoes that are moved by the wind. We stayed with them for one winter. Now we are returning to Kanata to live with our father."

The men spoke again among themselves. "You are not spirits of the dead?" they asked again.

"No. We are simply two brothers who have been away and we want to go home." The men waved, wished the brothers well, and quickly paddled back to shore.

The three ships sailed on, favoured with good winds at their backs. They were in the great river now; they could see both sides of it, were slowed by its massive, sweeping current. Cartier called it the Rivière Hochelaga. Five days later, they anchored in a secluded bay off a large wooded island. On shore, the brothers showed Cartier bushes loaded with nuts. "These are *quehaya*. Our people pick them for eating in the winter," Taignoagny told Cartier.

"We call them hazelnuts," said Cartier. "These taste much better than ours." And he named the island Ile aux Coudres in the French tongue, just as the Iroquois had done in theirs hundreds of years before.

The next day, as the wind slowly pushed the heavy ships upstream, the brothers paced from bow to stern, straining to be first to see their country.

Taignoagny won.

"There," he said excitedly to Cartier, pointing to the left and ahead at several small low wooded islands. "Those islands mark the beginning of Kanata."

CARTIER'S SECOND VOYAGE TO KANATA

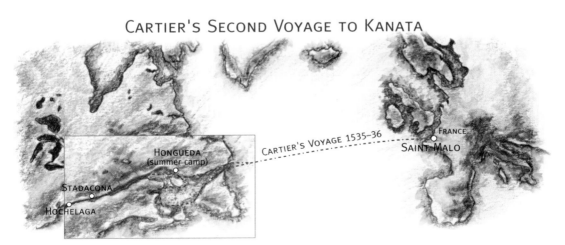

HONGUEDA
(summer camp)

STADACONA

HOCHELAGA

CARTIER'S VOYAGE 1535–36

FRANCE

SAINT-MALO

27

"Domagaya!" he called to his brother who was busy relieving himself over the ship's rail. "Look! I win!" Domagaya laughed, finished quickly and ran to join them. Straight ahead was a large island covered with trees tinged with autumn colours.

"Our people fish there," Domagaya told Cartier. When they anchored and went ashore, they saw a group of Iroquois. But when the people saw the strangers, they ran away.

"Haii," called Domagaya, and he spoke in Iroquois. "Don't be afraid. It's Taignoagny and Domagaya, the sons of Donnacona."

The people stopped, as if struck by lightning. One woman turned, her eyes grew wide, first in fear, then joy. "Haiieee," she cried. It was their aunt, Estahagao, Contarea's wife.

"It's them!" she cried to the others. "My nephews! They're alive!" Instantly, the two young men were surrounded by people laughing, hugging, touching their hands and faces to make sure that they were real. "Everyone thought you were dead," she said. "Except your father. He refused to let Contarea sing the death songs for you."

Cartier and his crew stood back and watched. Now the villagers rushed over and thanked them for returning the brothers safely. They brought eels and fish to their longboats, as well as gifts of corn and squash. "We are leaving," called Estahagao, "to tell your father that you are here."

The next morning, as the red glow of dawn appeared above the shuddering maples and soft white pines that lined the river, a dozen canoes appeared, paddling hard. It was Donnacona, members of the Bear clan and others. They had travelled all night.

Donnacona's canoe stopped at the first ship, *Emérillon*. "Haii," he called, the cry of a father looking for his long-lost sons.

The brothers heard it on board the *Grande Hermine* and ran to the rail. "He's here!" Domagaya cried.

The sailors on board *Emérillon* did not know what he wanted, did not know one savage from another. They waved him off. Donnacona moved toward the next ship. Then he saw them.

"Father!"

"Let's go," said Taignoagny and they scrambled over the rail and down to the longboat tied alongside. Donnacona stood as the others paddled, his arms raised in prayer and celebration, then waved to the boys and to Cartier who had come on deck.

"Father," the brothers called again as the canoe pulled close. They reached over, touched hands and hugged. And when they inhaled deeply his smell of wood smoke and buckskin, they knew that they were truly home and not in some long and awful dream.

Angoutenc, Contarea, Neguac and Miscou were all there. They touched each other, laughing. "You look like the strangers," Miscou said, seeing their French clothes, their long hair.

"You have grown," Donnacona said, grabbing each of his sons by the shoulder, looking them over. "Did Kart-yeh treat you well?"

Cartier was climbing down to join them in the longboat so Taignoagny said, "Yes, he took good care of us."

"They live in houses made of stone, Father," said Domagaya. "Beautiful houses and the light from the sun comes in through windows that are like ice that does not melt … "

He stopped. He could see the confusion on his father's face. Cartier climbed right into Donnacona's canoe. The Iroquois leader grabbed the captain's hands.

"Thank you for bringing my sons back to me," he said. Domagaya translated for his father.

"You now speak the strangers' tongue," said Donnacona.

"It is French. That is what these strangers calls themselves. They live in the country of France. We will tell you much more later."

"Come," said Cartier, "we must celebrate." He called to his crew to bring down wine and bread. "*Vive* Domagaya *et* Taignoagny," said the captain as he raised his pewter cup in both joy and relief at Donnacona's friendly reception. "*Vive* Kanata."

After all the Iroquois had wine and bread, Donnacona said, "Let's go back to our village. A feast is being prepared for you." The brothers quickly climbed up and retrieved the two bags of gifts they had brought.

"How far is your village?" asked Cartier. "Is there a place to anchor there?"

"A day's paddle," Domagaya answered. "Just past the end of this long island, on the north shore, you will see another river which joins this near our village. Perhaps your ships can go there." No one noticed Taignoagny's smile disappear.

With that they left. The two brothers sat in the bottom of the birchbark canoe that now seemed very small and fragile. To the sound of singing and laughter, they were carried home as heroes.

The moon was rising, almost full, the blood red moon of harvest, as their canoes approached the village. Huge fires of welcome burned on shore, the sweet smell of wood smoke filled the cool autumn air. Hundreds of people lined the bank, singing, banging drums, shaking rattles, their cattail torches flickering as people leapt and cheered.

Domagaya and Taignoagny had left more than a year ago in their moccasins. Now they stepped ashore in French-made shoes and disappeared into a seething mass of brown skin and buckskin, weaving among the swaying torches and dancing shadows, totally immersed in the sounds of joy. The brothers were too overwhelmed to speak, and for the first time in their lives knew what coming home really meant, and yet felt awkward in their French clothes and with all the new knowledge they had of the world and all the things they had seen. They did not understand these feelings, only knew them as vague, unsettling thoughts that lingered behind the excitement and joy.

They were swept up in a parade of people that carried them along a path through the trees, up a gently sloping hill, through towering fields of corn where even the corn cobs with their fine silky heads of hair seemed to nod their welcome. And then they were home. Shadows danced across the curved bark walls of the village longhouses. Before them, a dozen fires burned, and above these dangled roasts of deer and moose while clay pots simmered with stews and soups full of delicious smells. They were surrounded by the people with whom they had lived all their lives, except for those long, lonely months in France and the terrifying days at sea.

Donnacona stopped in front of their clan longhouse. The people crowded around, waiting. The bark curtain parted, and their grandmother, Sadeguenda, matron of the Bear clan emerged. Domagaya and Taignoagny grinned and ran to her. She stopped them short, grabbed Domagaya by the cheeks with her rough hands, stared long and hard into his eyes, then did the same with Taignoagny.

"Your Iroquois spirits are still with you." She nodded to each of them. "You are welcome to come home." Then she grabbed both their hands, holding them to her heart as her eyes squeezed shut. A single tear rolled down the dark crevices of her face.

"There will be time for talk later," called Donnacona to his people. "Let the feast begin."

The homecoming was exciting, yet vaguely unsettling.

The drum circle began the Welcoming Song as the brothers took the place of honour. Later when the dancing started, they eagerly joined in, uncomfortable with so much attention. Long after the moon set beyond the dark southern shore of the great river, long after everyone had eaten, the drumming, dancing and talk continued. For Domagaya and Taignoagny, everything old and familiar seemed new and strange, as if they had grown new eyes while they were away. Even the wooden eating bowls and wooden spoons seemed rough and crude compared to the French utensils. Yet they were very happy to be home.

cache
(KASH) a hiding place, usually a hole or a pit, for the storage of food, weapons or goods

The large council longhouse was packed. There was no room to sit, hardly room to stand. Everyone in the village who could squeeze in was there. Contarea shook his magic eagle stick and chanted prayers to the Great Spirit, thanked him for the harvest about to start, for the beautiful weather, the autumn moon, and the safe return of Domagaya and Taignoagny. The pipes were smoked. The time had come to hear the stories.

Donnacona rose and the crowd fell silent. He's grown older, thought Taignoagny. His eyes look tired.

"Since Kart-yeh took you away, there has been a heavy weight on the spirit of Kanata. Now that you are back, we can smile and laugh again. Though winter will soon be here, in my heart it feels that spring has come.

"Last year, we waited long into the autumn for Kart-yeh to bring you back to Hongueda. Then, with great sorrow we came back here for the harvest, to prepare for winter. We left a small party of warriors there in case you arrived. They almost froze to death paddling home through the snow and ice. They left a canoe, a tent, some warm skins and a cache of food for you.

"It was a long, sad winter in this village. We offered much tobacco to the spirits so they would make the visitors bring you back, but evil continued to haunt us. Twenty-one people died of a strange sickness we have not seen before. Our beloved Teandewiata went with them to the spirit world."

At this, the brothers bowed their heads, remembering their favourite sachem. The mood in the longhouse was sombre now, as in silence the people relived the bleak winter.

"Again this summer," Donnacona continued, "we travelled to Hongueda to fish and wait for you. When we arrived, we found the cache undisturbed. But there were many evil spirits, so we took down Cartier's cross and burned it, and we scattered the rocks and ashes to the four winds so there would be no sign of it. Then we moved our summer camp to a new place. Again, when you did not come, we left reluctantly. This time, I considered letting Contarea sing the death songs so that we could release you to the spirit world. Then, like a song sparrow, Estahagao arrived to say that three ships had come and that my two sons, two sons of this village, were on them."

At this, the agouhanna of Kanata raised his head and sang a song about his sons, a long song that began as sorrow and ended in thanksgiving. When he finished, there was a great murmur of appreciation for both the heartfelt truth of his story and the eloquence with which he told it. The Iroquois waited for the brothers to speak. Domagaya looked at Taignoagny. As the oldest, he would go first. And so he rose. In the dark council house, a sea of eager eyes waited in the firelight.

"Friends," he began. "Taignoagny and I are very happy to be home. We are grateful for the things you've said and done to welcome us. It seems a long time ago since the omen of the caribou that spoke from his wound with-out words. All of you who warned that this omen meant danger were right.

"Cartier, the French captain, is not a cruel man nor is he a warrior. But he is dangerous to our people. He has an agouhanna, a king, rich beyond your ability to imagine if you have not seen his wealth with your own eyes, yet who is greedy for more. Cartier lied to us when he put up his poles last summer at Hongueda. It is not a sign to help him sail his ships. Last winter, we learned the French tongue and found what that mark means." Domagaya stopped and swallowed.

"The poles make a shape called a cross. Many years ago, the son of their creator was tortured and killed on such a cross. Wherever they put one means they are claiming the land for their king and their creator. Cartier claimed ownership of Hongueda as French land last summer; that is what he told his king. They put a French name on it; they now call it New France."

The longhouse erupted with the news. Domagaya looked at Taignoagny, waiting for the bedlam to die down.

"That is the French way of claiming land. We have travelled with them on their ships for many weeks. Everywhere they go, they give a French name to every island, bay, point of land, river and stream and that is what they call it. They do not ask the Iroquois name. To them, it does not matter. They give it their own name and by doing so, they believe they not only found it, but that they own it. They are as greedy as starving bears who have stumbled upon a honeycomb."

"There is much to say, but the sun will soon be rising, and still Taignoagny needs to speak. I will tell you one more thing. Cartier is not that interested in our land. All he sees are rocks and trees and he grumbles. Why? He is looking for a way to sail across our land to another place far from here. In that land there are strange and valuable spices that the French use on their food. There is also special material that the French use to make fine shirts and clothes. The thread is made by worms."

Domagaya stopped, as this absurd idea sunk in and the room erupted in laughter. Domagaya shook his head.

"It is true. I have seen the shirts." Then he grew serious again. "The French have been to this land in their ships by another route, but it is not safe. It is a dangerous journey with many enemies who would attack them. So their king wants to find a shorter, safer passage to that land. That is why he paid for Cartier's three ships to come here. That is what they want. They are also looking for coloured metals, yellow and silver metals that have as much value in their land as wampum has in ours. Yet these French are not interested in our copper metal that we get from the Saguenay."

"That is enough for now. It is my brother's turn to speak."

Domagaya sat down as the longhouse buzzed. Taignoagny waited, then finally stood to take his turn.

"Friends," he began, and he pulled at his shirt. "We may be wearing French clothes but underneath beat Iroquois hearts." Great cheers and yelps. Then he pulled his shirt over his head and threw it onto the dirt floor. There was a gasp from the crowd.

"This son of Kanata is home," he said, almost spitting out the words. The crowd yelled and cheered.

"My brother has perhaps been kind to the French with his words, but I want to tell you that they are evil people. In their country, people who do not believe in their creator are tied to a pole and burned." Taignoagny paused, waited for the commotion to die down.

"Will they do the same to us?" he asked, his eyes flashing. The room suddenly was very quiet.

"The French are powerful and very rich. They have many ships like the ones on our river, as many as there are stars in the sky, I'm told. On those ships, they have giant black thundersticks so heavy it takes ten men to carry them. With one shot from one of these cannon, they could knock down this longhouse and kill us all."

Again a storm of sound rose, then fell.

wampum (WAM-pum) small, cylindrical beads made from polished shells that were widely used as currency by North American cultures. The word has also been used in a slang sense to mean money.

"The French live in stone houses with straight walls and pointed roofs. They have many rooms full of beautiful things for sitting on and sleeping on. They wear many clothes in summer, as if it was winter. They eat wonderful food with fine metal spoons and metal plates. Each family lives in its own house. They own this home and they believe they own the land it sits on. Many are very rich, yet they do not share. People with no food can starve outside a home where there is plenty. Sometimes, they will throw a dried crust of bread to a beggar. But often, they will beat him and drive him off.

"And ..." he paused. "They beat their children."

At this, a huge cry of outrage welled up. Touching a child in discipline showed the shameful failure of parents.

"There is one more thing to say," Taignoagny continued. "The French have a word for us. They call us 'sauvages'. They think we are like animals, that we are stupid. That is why they give us gifts that have little value in their country. They laugh at us when they see how happy we are with ribbons and beads. Even the knives they give us are not as good as theirs. They call them trinkets, toys, and think we are children for liking them."

A low grumbling ran through the room.

"There is much more to tell, but I have told you the things we need to think about now. Cartier and his three ships are at our eastern door. They want Domagaya and me to take them up the great river to Hochelaga. We said we would because we were their captives. But now that we are free and at home, I don't want to do this. I'm afraid we will be captured again and taken back to France. You must tell us what to do." And he sat down.

quandary
(KWAN-da-ree) a state
of uncertainty,
a dilemma

$\mathbf{D}$omagaya heaved a deep sigh. It had taken only a few days to slip back into his old life. The welcoming feast had lasted three days, a joyful time. The brothers had spoken at the village council for three long nights. But their words alarmed the people of Kanata, throwing them into a quandary. The Iroquois were even more mistrustful of Cartier now, more frightened, too.

"We will act as if nothing has changed," Donnacona said. "Let us wait and see what Kart-yeh and his men do." One thing was certain: the brothers would not go back on Cartier's ship, would not guide him to Hochelaga.

Domagaya, Taignoagny, their father and twenty-five canoes then left the village for a few days, while the women harvested the corn. They slipped to the south side of the big island, followed the southern shore of the great river as it flowed east, passed by Cartier's sleeping ships in the dark. They went down river to a group of islands to fish, hunt and gather nuts for winter. Now with canoes full, they were ready to head back.

"I wonder what that devil Cartier's been doing?" Taignoagny said later, as they paddled upstream toward their village. Domagaya was surprised at his brother's anger toward the Frenchman. Taignoagny had shaved his head, leaving just his topknot in the village style, and wore a new deerskin shirt and breeches. Domagaya still wore his French clothes; his hair was still long, too. He was proud of his new status, of being noticed, especially by the young women in the village.

When the Iroquois got to the big island, the French ships were gone. "Let's get back quickly," Donnacona said. As they raced home and rounded the point where the two rivers meet, they saw Cartier's three ships at anchor.

Donnacona waved and called to Cartier as they approached. The Frenchman came to the rail of his ship, waved back. "Come up," he called as Donnacona and several others pulled alongside. "Come for some wine and food." Domagaya and Taignoagny kept their canoe back. They saw Cartier look around and finally spot them.

"Domagaya. Taignoagny, come, come." He smiled and waved them over. But the brothers kept their distance, did not return his smiles or waves. Cartier's own smile disappeared. "You are coming with us to Hochelaga as you promised, no?" The Frenchman looked up at the sky. "We will be leaving soon."

"Yes, yes," Domagaya lied. "Of course we will take you there. In a few days when you are ready." Cartier shrugged as they abruptly turned and paddled away.

The next day, the brothers were on the banks of the great river with their father and some villagers. Cartier and a group of French sailors approached, many carrying guns.

"Good morning," Donnacona greeted the Frenchman.

"Good morning," Cartier replied. "It's a beautiful fall day."

"Yes," said the agouhanna. "Soon the land will sleep under the blanket of winter."

"Cartier," interrupted Taignoagny. "Why is it when your men are working, they still carry so many guns like a war party? My father finds this rude. As you can see, we don't carry our weapons here unless we are going off to hunt."

Cartier smiled at Donnacona who, of course, did not understand a word of what his son had said in French. But Cartier's eyes hardened when he spoke to Taignoagny. "My son, as you know very well, it is our custom to carry our weapons. We do this in France and we will do it here. We do not mean to offend anyone, but we are in a new land and we will carry our guns to protect ourselves." Taignoagny abruptly turned and left, Domagaya behind him.

Donnacona watched his sons go, turned back to Cartier. "I want us to

Autumn sunrises seem to set the maple forests afire on the great island of Kanata, just east of what was once Stadacona. Today it bears the name the French gave it, Île d'Orléans.

be brothers," he said. "In friendship and trade. You, the great France leader and I, agouhanna of Kanata, will make a pact." Cartier nodded, without understanding.

Donnacona reached for the captain's right hand. Cartier, thinking he wanted to shake hands, extended his. But Donnacona took it, opened it palm upward. Then he pulled out his knife, opened his own right palm, and drew his knife across it. A red line of blood appeared. He handed his knife to Cartier, motioned for him to cut his own hand. Cartier hesitated, looked at his men, then gingerly slid the knife along his palm. No blood appeared. He looked up at Donnacona, then did it again harder, faster. This time, there was blood. Donnacona nodded, smiled, then grabbed Cartier's bloody hand, held it with his own. "Now we are brothers," Donnacona said. With that, the villagers around cheered three times. Cartier smiled uncertainly, looked at his cut hand, then turned to go back to his ship.

"Why did you do that?" Taignoagny demanded later. He was furious. They were eating with their father in the clan longhouse. Donnacona pulled a fish head out of his wooden bowl and sucked the eyes out with a slurping sound. A bloody strip of hide was wrapped around his right hand.

"You watch that angry tongue of yours." Donnacona's eyes flashed.

Domagaya lowered his head in shame. He'd never seen anyone question his father before, certainly not a son. It was not the Iroquois way. Perhaps the French way, he remembered.

"It is not wise to have Kart-yeh angry with us; he is very powerful." Donnacona leaned forward and spit fish bones into the fire. "Their long guns can kill us any time. Their cannons can knock down our longhouses. We want to trade with these French. If they are angry with Kanata, they will trade with Hochelaga instead. We must persuade Kart-yeh not to go to Hochelaga but we must not make him angry. Do you understand, Taignoagny?"

Taignoagny nodded, his head bowed, although his mouth was tightly shut, a thin grim line. "I will not be questioned any more by you," Donnacona continued. "You have learned some bad manners from the French." And he got up and left the longhouse. The French were busy. Three longboats full of men pulled hard on their oars, the *Grande Hermine* behind them on a long rope. Slowly, with much yelling and cursing, they towed the ship into the shallow water at the mouth of the little river. They ran a line to shore, pulled it until the ship came aground in the muddy sand. The huge ship seemed even bigger as the tall masts towered above

CARTIER'S WINTER FORT 1535-36

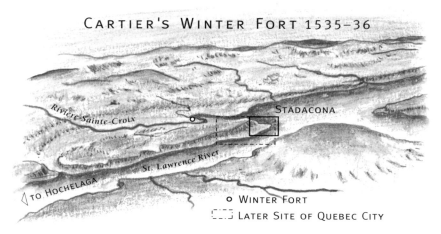

Rivière-Sainte-Croix

STADACONA

St. Lawrence River

TO HOCHELAGA

○ WINTER FORT

⌐‐⌐ LATER SITE OF QUEBEC CITY

the trees. The French beached the *Petite Hermine* in the same way beside her sister ship. As the tide went out, the two ships settled on the bottom. Hundreds of villagers watched, fascinated.

"Why are they bringing this ship in here?" they asked. "Is there a storm coming?" They scanned the skies but could see nothing in the blue autumn sky.

"Let's find out what these French are doing," Donnacona said to several sachem.

Once again, Cartier invited Donnacona, his sons and village sachem on board. He and the French gentlemen greeted them warmly, gave them food and wine and some small gifts. "These are in gratitude for allowing us to put our ships here," Cartier told Donnacona as Domagaya translated.

"Then you are not going to Hochelaga? Donnacona asked.

Cartier's smiled disappeared. "No, we are still going to Hochelaga. That's why we've left the small ship, *Emérillon*, out there at anchor."

"My father is annoyed that you insist on going up the river," Taignoagny interjected. "There is nothing much to see there except a few islands." His voice hardened. "He does not want Domagaya or me to go with you."

Cartier laughed scornfully. "Well, you and your brother promised that you'd go and now you're breaking your promise?" He shrugged. "I'm sorry. My agouhanna has ordered me to go to Hochelaga and so I must push on and explore this river for my king and my country. I'll give you presents if you change your mind."

"We will not be bought with your trinkets," Taignoagny snapped. "I will not go." He climbed over the side and left. Donnacona smiled grimly, shook Cartier's hand. The meeting was over.

The council fire burned late that night. "We must not anger the French." Agona, the war sachem, was speaking. "It would be like hitting a hornets' nest with a stick. We will be sorry." Some sachem nodded in agreement. "Perhaps they will not form an alliance or trade agreement with Hochelaga. But we cannot stop them if they do. If would be foolish to try." He sat down.

Contarea rose to speak. "Our agouhanna has made a blood pact with Kart-yeh who is now his brother." He looked directly at Taignoagny and Domagaya. "He was wise to make that pact." The two young men lowered their eyes. "But perhaps Kart-yeh does not fully understand what we mean. We need to make some gifts to him to make our pact stronger." He paused. "We should give him some children."

Angoutenc rose quickly. "Our shaman speaks wisely. This is a difficult time for us. We must tread softly and act with generosity. The French, of course, have no children for trade but they have given us many gifts. I think a gift of children is a good idea."

Donnacona stood. "Let me be the first to offer a son. We will give him Miscou, the son of Neguac."

Contarea rose quickly. "We will offer him Manuoane, daughter of Estahagao. She has seen twelve winters and although she is small she will be a woman soon."

Taignoagny looked at Domagaya and scowled. "This is crazy. Our own brother and cousin," he whispered. "Now they will go to France as captives and live as we lived."

"You can't do anything about it," Domagaya warned. "Our father will lose face if you speak out." Another sachem stood up and offered his young son, Zisto. And it was done. The next morning, the Iroquois paraded to the French ships in their new place on the shore. They carried baskets of eel and mackerel as gifts. Donnacona hailed Cartier and, as he and his men stepped ashore, the people of Kanata sang and cheered. Donnacona drew a large circle in the sand and gently pushed the Frenchmen into it. They smiled but clutched their guns tightly. Donnacona drew a straight line in the sand and told his people to stand behind it. He motioned for a young girl with red eyes to come forward.

"Kart-yeh," he began. "You are a good friend." He waited for Domagaya to translate, then continued as Cartier nodded. "I present this young girl child as a gift to mark our friendship and our blood pact." Donnacona led the girl to Cartier and made her step inside the circle. The crowd cheered and yelled. Cartier seemed mystified.

"This line in the sand is our Mother Earth," Donnacona continued. "The circle in which you stand is the sun. Your coming is like a new light shining on the people of Kanata. You have brought us many gifts and great knowledge. In return I present you with these boys, also as a sign of our friendship, which will last as long as the sun shines." One by one, the agouhanna took Miscou and Zisto by the hand, put them inside the circle with Cartier and his Frenchmen. Miscou's lower lip trembled. Zisto sucked his thumb. He was four and didn't understand what was happening. Donnacona smiled, shook Cartier's hand again as the villagers cheered.

Cartier looked puzzled as he spoke. "My friend, Donnacona, agouhanna of the great village of Kanata, you honour me with these precious gifts. Thank you."

Taignoagny could contain his anger no longer. "That girl is the daughter of our father's sister," he said, stepping forward and pointing to Manuoane. "And this boy is our brother, our father's son from his Mi'kmaq wife. He has given you these children so that you will not go to Hochelaga, that you will stay here and respect our father's wishes."

Cartier's smiled disappeared. "Then tell your father he must take these children back. Nothing will stop me from continuing to Hochelaga. Those are orders from my king and I will obey them."

Domagaya was horrified at his brother's rudeness. "Monsieur Cartier, please, my father his given you his own child and his own niece out of the great affection he has for you." He paused, turned, looked Taignoagny in the eye as he spoke. "I will go with you to Hochelaga. I will show you the way."

Taignoagny grabbed his brother by the shoulder. "What are you doing? You, you are a traitor."

Domagaya threw off his brother's arm, jabbed him with his finger. "You have disgraced our father in front of Cartier. You have shamed him in the eyes of our people. It is you who are the traitor. You have no right to interfere." Domagaya's fists clenched, storm clouds roiled across his eyes.

The two brothers stood face to face like hissing raccoons. Taignoagny spit on the sand at Domagaya's feet, turned and left.

The search for a passage to China, and the lure of the unknown, drew the French and other Europeans ever westward into North America.

Cartier smiled at Domagaya, then ordered the children to be taken on board the *Grande Hermine*. His sailors came back with two swords and two metal wash basins. One after another, Cartier handed these to Donnacona. "I give you these, monsieur, in gratitude for your hospitality and friendship."

Donnacona's eyes shone as he handled each sword, withdrew the long blade from its scabbard. "Thank you, Kart-yeh." He looked at the captain. "To mark this occasion, would you fire the big guns on your ships? My sons have told me about them but we have not heard them."

Cartier agreed and ordered his crew to aim twelve cannons into the woods and fire on his command. When they were ready, Cartier drew his own sword, held it high, then dropped it. Instantly, the air was filled with a terrible thunder. The Iroquois yelped and cried. Many dropped to the sand. Clouds of white smoke poured from the cannons as if they were giant pipes.

Suddenly, a young man from the village ran onto the beach. "The French have killed two of our people," he yelled. "They fired the guns on the ship out on the river and killed them." The man ran back into the trees.

Hearing this the Iroquois ran back to their village, Donnacona and Domagaya behind them, leaving the French standing on the beach. When they got back to the village, they found that no one had been shot. It was a trick by the angry Taignoagny.

Domagaya and Taignoagny argued into the evening. They argued in the longhouse until the women shushed them out. They fought and wrestled in the cornfield, knocking over the ripe stocks. They jumped into the river to wash and fought there. Later, as they returned to eat, exhausted, Donnacona was waiting for them.

"Domagaya, listen to me," he began. "You have a special place in the hearts of our people. That is because you are my son, and also because people look well on you and have watched you grow into a fine young man. Your journey with Kart-yeh has taught you much. But knowledge is not wisdom. The Council of Kanata has decided. We do not want Kart-yeh to go to Hochelaga and make an alliance with them. We want these French to trade with us, to give us long guns so we can protect ourselves from the Toudamans and have independence from Hochelaga. That is why the elders do not want you to go there with Kart-yeh. Do you understand?" Domagaya nodded but inside he was hurt that the council and his father had sided with Taignoagny, who had behaved so badly. "People in the village are beginning to talk. They see that you wear your French clothes and that your hair is cut in the French way. Are you no longer an Iroquois? I have lost one son today. I have no wish to lose another."

The young man winced.

"Come boys," Donnacona, seeing that his words had hit home. "Contarea has a plan to scare these French away from Hochelaga."

Cartier had moved to the *Emérillon* anchored in the great river. The next morning, a group of Iroquois went to the river and waited in the woods, out of sight of Cartier and his men. Then, Donnacona, his sons and villagers came out from hiding and walked to the shore.

"Haii," Taignoagny called to Cartier, as if nothing had happened the day before.

"Good day," replied Cartier coolly from the ship's rail. "Would you like me to send the longboat over?"

"Not now," came the reply, "but soon."

At that moment, a strange apparition appeared. Three devils with long horns on their heads, black faces, and covered in dog skins, came down the river in a canoe. The devils faced the shore, away from the French ship, and as they got close one of the beings raised his voice and made awful sounds. Their canoe ground into the shore and suddenly, the three fell down as if they were dead. Donnacona and the villagers quickly carried them and their canoe into the woods. One of the devils, Contarea in disguise, rose and with the other two shamans, made great long speeches about the horrible dangers that lay ahead on the river. In loud voices, they announced that the winter spirit would soon be here and would wreack vengeance on any one who dared go to the cursed country of Hochelaga. It was a masterful performance.

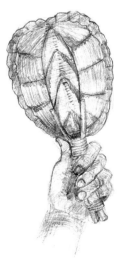

Now it was Taignoagny's and Domagaya's turn. The two brothers walked out of the woods toward the river, holding hands. "Jesus, Jesus, Jesus," Taignoagny cried, his eyes raised to the sky as he had seen in France. He checked quickly to see if Cartier was on deck. He was.

"Jesus, Mary, Jacques Cartier," cried Domagaya, his eyes raised skyward, too, as they reached the shore opposite the ship.

"What is it?" called Cartier. "Has something happened?"

There is bad news.

"There is bad news," cried Taignoagny. "Very bad news." And the two brothers cried and called to heaven once again.

"What's the problem?" Cartier's face was filled with mock concern but there was a twinkle in his eyes.

"Our God, Cudouagny, has appeared at Hochelaga and he has sent three men to deliver the news, very bad news." Taignoagny fell to his knees in the sand, his palms together as if in prayer.

Domagaya continued. "Cudouagny has warned that he is angry and will send much snow and ice down on Hochelaga so that all men will perish."

Cartier and his men roared. "Your god is a fool," said Cartier, almost doubled over with laughter. "You should tell his messengers that he doesn't know what he's saying."

"You should have learned in France that our Jesus will keep us safe from the cold, if you put your faith in him."

At this, Taignoagny and Domagaya stood. "Have you spoken to your Jesus?" Taignoagny asked.

"My priests speak to him every day. Jesus told them that the weather ahead will be fine."

"We will tell the others," the brothers replied. The battle of the gods was over.

"Keep your canoes out of sight. I don't want those sharp-eyed French to see you." Donnacona was speaking to eight of the village's best young warriors. "If they see you, just pretend you're fishing or hunting." The spies nodded. "When you come back, we want to hear about everything they did. Go now. May the Great Spirit protect you."

When the high tide came in the next morning, the *Emérillon* and two longboats full of Frenchmen left for Hochelaga. Hours before them, unnoticed, two canoes had slipped away from Kanata and paddled west ahead of them. The rest of the French sailors and the Iroquois children stayed on board the two large ships aground in the little river.

"We are going hunting," announced Donnacona as he strode into the longhouse. He and Neguac had taken some smoked fish and cornbread to Miscou, Manuoane and Zisto. They'd had to tear themselves away from the children for all three were crying. Taignoagny and Domagaya were still lying

In the early light of dawn, two canoes slip past the Emérillon.

on their sleeping platforms, under warm sleeping skins. "We will go for ten, maybe fourteen nights," Donnacona added. "I want to go now."

Hearing the tension in their father's voice they scrambled out of bed. He'd lost face by failing to stop Cartier from leaving for Hochelaga and needed a diversion, for himself as much as for his people. Two weeks in the bush would be good for everyone. Besides, hunting was necessary with winter coming. Great wreaths of mist now played on the river every morning.

Thirty canoes of hunters, women and children launched into the little river and turned north, toward the lakes and forest of their traditional hunting territory, toward the land of the Saguenay.

Maybe when we get back Cartier and his French will have left for home, Taignoagny thought. But there was something gnawing in his gut, something bad. Then, he remembered: the dead buck talking without words. He shook his head, shaking the thought away, and leaned harder into his paddling.

They travelled far into the northern forest and pitched their small skin hunting tents by a beautiful lake surrounded with brilliant gold and red leaves of autumn. The Great Spirit, Cudouagny, was happy with his people and hunting went well. Domagaya and Taignoagny, however, were still wary of each other and went off every day in different directions to stalk caribou at twilight, shoot moose wading in the shallow marshes, or trap sleek beaver in their ponds. The weather was clear. The spirits of the dead played across the sky above them every night.

"Tell us more about this France," Angoutenc said to Domagaya one night as they sat around the fire after a meal of fresh venison and porcupine. "About their agouhanna."

Domagaya began slowly. "Well, one time Cartier took us to see him; they call him Frans-wah. It was a long journey. The French have these animals called horses which are as big as moose but without horns or a hump. They are quite tame; I have sat on one myself. They tie two of these horses to a wooden box that has circles under it so that it can be pulled over their trails. We sat inside this black box while a man sat on top and pulled on cords attached to the horses' mouths. When the man pulled on the right side of the horses' mouths, they turned right; if he pulled on the left side, the horses turned left. They have special

spirits of the dead
in this instance, a reference to the northern lights

words to make the horses go faster or to make them stop. This is how we travelled to see their king."

"We should try these tricks with moose," one woman said. The group roared.

"We rode in this carriage to the main village in the country," Domagaya continued, "which is called Pah-ree. It is many, many times bigger than Kanata or even Hochelaga. There is a palisade around this village made of stone and every night the king's warriors walk around it with bows and arrows to protect the people."

His listeners nodded their heads.

"The people in this village all live in stone long-houses that are built side by side so close they touch each other. In the centre of this village there is one longhouse that is so big you can see it from far away. This is where their god lives."

"They built a house for their god!"

"Did you see their god?"

"No, like Cudouagny, he can't be seen, but I saw many pictures of his wife, Mary. Their god made her pregnant without lying with her and they had a boy named Jesus. He was a shaman and had much magic but he was tortured and killed anyway. They carve stone pictures that look like Mary and Jesus. These are in the longhouses where their god lives. They have a longhouse for him in every village in the country where people go to talk to him, but they only have one god."

"He's the only god?"

Domagaya shrugged. "That's what they say."

"Who looks after the hunters?"

"And the fish?"

"What about the corn?"

"This god looks after everything; that's what Cartier said."

"You haven't told us about their agouhanna yet," reminded one of the listeners just as Taignoagny strolled over, picking his teeth with a stick.

"Why don't you tell them?" Domagaya said to his brother.

"He is not much of a king," shrugged Taignoagny, sitting down across the fire from Domagaya. "He's certainly not a warrior." He grabbed a stick and poked the fire, warming himself to his story.

palisade
(PAL-is-sade) a tall fence of poles or stone joined to form a fortification

49

He talked long into the night about the king's great house with its square stone walls and shining stone floors, about the fine clothes he wore, his crown of yellow metal with its glittering red and green stones, about the big chair he sat in, the men and women who surrounded him always, woman in flowing robes that pushed out their breasts, which were white as snow.

He told how Cartier had given them a deer hide and ordered them to make new buckskin loin cloths, how they wore them when they saw the king, how they had made war paint, too, and put that on. He talked of how they made bows and arrows and showed the king inside his house how they hunted by shooting a white bird that sat on a carved stone woman, not Mary but someone else. All these things he told the Iroquois. And years later, the people would tell these stories to their grandchildren word for word, just as they had been told. When the loons out on the misty lake fell silent, Taignoagny ended his story. The Iroquois crawled into their small hunting tents, wrapped themselves in furry hides, and dreamed strange dreams of places far away.

S omething was wrong. The lead canoes stopped; the people in them pointed at the shore. Donnacona paddled harder. After two weeks of hunting, they were almost home. He rounded the bend in the little river, then he, too, stopped suddenly, letting the canoe drift down to the others. He barely heard the angry yells behind him, his sons, paddling hard.

"Those French witches," someone said.

"How dare they do this?"

How dare they do this?

The two French ships were still there, beached. But close by, on the level land in front of them, a stone's throw from shore, stood something new and awful: a palisade, a huge rectangular fortification of fresh-cut spruce logs, each log with a sharpened point. Frenchmen with guns stood on platforms behind these poles. In some places, where the poles were cut away, the black round mouths of cannons poked out.

"There's a longhouse inside," said Domagaya as his canoe brushed his father's. A column of smoke rose from the stones at one end of a peaked log roof behind the palisade. On a tall, thin pole, the French flag curled out in the chill October breeze. They could see one small door in the fort; it faced the ships and it was closed.

"Why would they build such a place?" asked Donnacona almost to himself, despair in his voice.

Taignoagny paddled up in time to hear the question. Through gritted teeth, he spoke the answer they all knew. "They are staying here all winter."

"We must kill these dogs." Angoutenc said, his dark eyes narrowed. "They have rubbed our hospitality in our face. We will burn this fort and their two ships. Tonight!"

"No!" said Donnacona. "Not yet, anyway. Let's get to our village. Perhaps something has happened."

The village was safe. The women had taken in the harvest. The rafters in the longhouses were thick with corn, hanging to dry. The pumpkins and squash were buried in deep storage pits dug in the far ends of the longhouses. The spies had just returned, too. Cartier would be back tomorrow or the next day, they said. Donnacona invited them to the council to report.

"We kept ahead of them as you instructed." Hebbehin, the leader of the eight warriors, stood before the sachem and elders. "We warned the agouhanna at Achelacy that the French were coming. He gave Kart-yeh gifts of two children, but Kart-yeh only kept one, a girl, I think. When the French got to the islands at the end of the lake, they could sail no farther against the current. So they left their ship and some men and continued in their two longboats rowing."

"Ouchidasca, agouhanna of Hochelaga, had already heard of Kart-yeh. He invited us to stay and we pretended to be with his people. He greeted Kart-yeh warmly. Ouchidasca wanted the Frenchman to heal his crippled arms and legs and Kart-yeh touched them but nothing happened. He gave them all knives and rings and other gifts he has given to us. Then he made a speech while he looked at some marks in a black thing he held open in his hands."

Hebbehin stopped. "To us, Kart-yeh did not seem the same as when he is here. He seemed frightened. His men held their guns as if expecting an attack at any minute. Yet they went inside the village palisades and looked in their longhouses. Then they walked up the mountain where the spirits live but only stayed a little while. When he came down, Kart-yeh and his men refused to eat even though a feast had been prepared."

A rumble filled the longhouse. The Iroquois could not believe how rude these Frenchmen were to turn down generous hospitality, though they had seen this before.

"The French, they almost ran to their longboats." Hebbehin broke into a smile as he remembered. The Iroquois laughed. It was good to know that this powerful Frenchman was afraid of them. "We passed them easily in the night as we came home. Perhaps they will be here tomorrow or the next day." Hebbehin nodded to Donnacona. "Ouchidasca sends you greetings and looks forward to a visit this winter." Then he sat down.

Angoutenc rose and turned to Hebbehin. "You are saying that Kart-yeh did not make a treaty or pact with Ouchidasca?" He seemed surprised.

Hebbehin rose to answer, shook his head. "No. Ouchidasca told him about the rapids on the river past Hochelaga that Kart-yeh had seen from the mountain. They also talked about copper metal and the Saguenay and about gold metal. But they made no pact."

A gust of wind hissed across the roof of the longhouse, rattling a loose piece of bark. The reed torches inside swooped and flickered, chasing shadows across the faces. Donnacona rose to speak.

"You bring us good news, Hebbehin. You men have done your job well." There were murmurs of agreement. "But there is still the matter of this palisade and pointy house that Kart-yeh has built. Angoutenc." Donnacona invited the war sachem to speak.

"Let's kill them all tonight before Kart-yeh returns." He looked around. "We'll use flaming arrows to burn the fort and the ships, then shoot them as they come running out like ants."

"But the French will still have one ship left," said Agona, standing, "and it has many cannons as well as guns. If what Domagaya and Taignoagny say is true, those cannons could knock all our longhouses down and kill all our women and children, too."

"It is true these French are rude and greedy creatures." Sadeguenda looked worried as she spoke. "But if we kill them, will not more come across the sea and avenge their deaths? They have many ships and many guns. We cannot win such a war."

Contarea rose. "This talk of guns and war is no good. Kart-yeh may be many things but, as Domagaya has said, he is not a warrior. He could have killed us at any time and he has not." The discussion went on, each person voicing a point of view. Finally, Donnacona rose.

"As I listen to this talk, I remember the words of our wise old friend, Teandewiata, who now is in the spirit world. Remember his words after the omen? 'They have accomplished things our people have not dreamed of,' he told us. 'I want to see them before I die. Not just to satisfy the curiosity of an old man, but that we may learn from them and make better lives for ourselves, for our children and their children. Perhaps we can make a treaty with them that will bring us wealth and weapons that will protect us from our enemies. Friends, we should not be afraid of the days yet to come for we might as well run from the rising sun.'"

He stopped, letting the words rest in the minds of the listeners. "His words are just as wise today as they were last year. If we kill this Frenchman who is much respected and very powerful in his country, we may start a war we cannot win. I have made a blood pact of friendship with him and I would lose my honour. Our people of Kanata would lose the wealth we might gain through trade; we could never use those guns for hunting. Our women would never have fine sharp knives and other things. I would not be a good agouhanna if I let these things happen. I am angry, too, but let us not take action against these French. Let us be guided by the spirit of wise Teandewiata whose words live still in our hearts."

The Iroquois became actors again, swallowing their anger over the fort and greeting Cartier warmly when he arrived two days later. He seemed relieved to be back and gave out many presents to the villagers. Cartier had never visited their village so Donnacona invited him. The Frenchman came with his armed men. Inside the longhouse, hanging on a pole that supported a sleeping platform, Donnacona pointed to five topknots hanging from a cord.

"What are they?" asked Cartier.

"Scalps of the Toudamans," Donnacona replied. "They massacred our people two years ago near Saguenay on the way to Hongueda. We avenge these deaths whenever we can." Cartier frowned. Shortly afterward they left and returned to the safety of their fort.

The message had been delivered.

A few days later, the Iroquois sent another message: they stopped supplying the Frenchmen with fresh eels and fish.

"You two did this, you rogues," Cartier called to Domagaya and Taignoagny one day as he entered the fort. "You are *agojuda*, very bad."

Taignoagny smirked. "Perhaps if you gave our people more than trinkets, they would not feel so cheated."

Winter along the lower St. Lawrence brings deep snow and long months of cold, so the spring thaw is always greatly anticipated.

Shortly after that, Manuoane escaped from the *Grande Hermine* and ran back to Contarea and Estahagao. The anxious Cartier reacted quickly. His men added horizontal poles to the palisades, then dug deep ditches around the fort at the base of the walls. They built a bridge across the ditch that could be raised and lowered. Every time he and his men went out, they were heavily armed. The French now stood guard on the palisade platforms all night and sounded horns when they changed.

"Why are you doing this?" Domagaya called out one day as he and a group of friends passed by.

"You know why," replied Cartier. "You are troublemakers. You persuaded the girl to run away. Your heads are filled with evil thoughts. But I might forgive you if you bring her back."

A few days later Donnacona, Domagaya and Taignoagny returned with Manuoane and took her to the ship. "The cabin boys beat me; that is why I ran away," she told Cartier as Domagaya translated. Pleased that the issue was settled and friendship restored, Cartier broke out the wine and food. They toasted in the French custom as large snowflakes fell.

It seemed the snow would never stop. When it did, huge winds sprang up and blizzards raged down the great river and turned the powdery mounds into huge drifts against the Iroquois longhouses and against the French palisades. The *Grande Hermine, Petite Hermine* and the *Emérillon* were soon frozen in the shallow river. Then one day, it warmed and rains came, encasing everything in ice. At night, the woods rang with the sound of tree branches snapping. By late November, the moose were starving and disappeared deep into the woods. With game scarce, the hunters went farther and farther, bringing back less and less to their hungry families.

In December, the sickness struck.

Domagaya awoke one night and heard it. A honking cough. Not the friendly sound of geese, but something rough and rasping like trees rubbing in the wind. The cough and fever ripped through Angoutenc's longhouse. Within a week, five of his family were dead. A few days later, the great warrior himself died.

Contarea sang his death song, as his two wives wailed and lashed themselves with grief. They wrapped Angoutenc's body in bark with his bow, arrows and knife and filled his tobacco pouch for the journey. Domagaya and Taignoagny helped carry his body to the cemetery, trudging through the drifts in their snowshoes. The wind tore at the fur robes of the Iroquois as they hoisted Angoutenc to his death platform high up on four poles. As a muffled drum beat slowly, they offered more prayers to the Great Spirit, Cudouagny. Angoutenc's first wife tied a turtle shell to the platform as a sign of their clan, then the mourners filed by and put tobacco in it.

As Taignoagny turned to leave the cemetery, something caught his eye. A blue scrap waving in the wind from a death platform. He went to look at it. It was Teandewiata's trade blanket. A wave of sadness swept over him. What have we done to make the spirits so angry with us?

The French were miserable and shivered in their thin clothes but they were not dying. Perhaps their god was not so angry with them, the Iroquois said. They didn't see much of them, but could hear them at work on their ships, hammering, pounding ceaselessly. Smoke rose from the ovens on their ships and the villagers' stomachs ached at the delicious smell of fresh French bread. Perhaps they have better medicine, the Iroquois said.

The people of Stadacona were running out of food. "We must go hunting," Donnacona announced one cold February day. "We'll go by canoe; there is too much snow in the bush." The salt water and tides in the great river often kept a channel open all winter. Donnacona, Taignoagny and several others left the next day, bundled in heavy fur mitts and robes. Domagaya could not go with them. He was sick.

At first Domagaya was afraid he, too, would die. His left knee was swollen to the size of a baby. He'd been in bed a week and could hardly walk. His teeth were loose; his gums were black. "Ugh," Neguac said one day, "your breath smells like dead skunk. I'll make some medicine." She came back soon with branches of white cedar, stripped off the nee- dles, threw them into the tea-making pot, boiled them for a long time. "Drink this," she said. "It is an annedda potion. You'll be better soon." She paused, then added. "We have lost almost forty people now. From a different sickness."

Neguac was right. Within a week of taking the bitter tea Domagaya was better. The soreness in his mouth was gone. He went for a walk, squinting in the bright sunlight after spending so much time in the longhouse.

"What? I see that you're well," exclaimed Cartier when he saw Domagaya down by the river. "You were very sick just a few days ago. How did you recover so quickly? Domagaya told him about Neguac's medicine. "My servant caught the same disease when he was visiting your father's house," said Cartier slyly. "Perhaps she can show us how to make this tea for him."

"I'll send her," Domagaya replied. That afternoon, Neguac and Estahagao came to Cartier's ship and led him to a tall cedar tree. They stripped branches off and told him how to make the tea. A week later, the French had cut the tree down and stripped its branches clean. "Perhaps the French are sicker than we thought," Domagaya said to Neguac. That annedda tree, of course, would never heal anyone again.

There were more deaths in March as the spring blizzards struck. There were fifty new bodies on platforms in the Iroquois cemetery and it was whis- pered that the French, too, were dying. Mysterious mounds of snow were piled high against the walls inside the fort. Perhaps they were hiding their dead until spring.

Charles and Jean wait outside Donnacona's lodge.

Donnacona returned in mid-April. His two-week hunting trip had turned into two months. "We went as far as Hochelaga," he explained to Domagaya as they unloaded frozen chunks of deer and moose from the canoes. "Ouchidasca called a grand council meeting," he added. "We discussed the Toudamans and the French." He wouldn't say more except that sixty Hochelagans had returned with him.

"Are we going to kill Cartier before he leaves?" Domagaya asked.

Donnacona hesitated, then spoke. "The ice is melting and Kart-yeh's ships will soon be free. I am worried that he will seize more of our people and take them to France. But Taignoagny and I have a plan. We will tell you about it later."

Cartier must have worried about the appearance of strangers in the village, because he did something unexpected. He sent two of his men, Charles and Jean, to visit Donnacona. These men were well-liked in the village, but they had never come alone before. "Tell them I'm sick in bed," Donnacona told Neguac when he heard the Frenchmen were at his door. So the men searched for Taignoagny and found him in another longhouse, filled with strangers.

"Come," said Taignoagny when he saw Cartier's men and quickly whisked them out.

"Why are those people here?" the one called Charles asked.

Taignoagny shrugged. "They are just visiting." He led the men half-way back to their ships and turned to go. "I want Cartier to do a favor for me," he said. "I want him to seize one of our sachem, Agona. He has done something against me and I want Cartier to take him back to France. I would be very pleased."

"We'll pass the message to him," they said. When Cartier heard the request, he sent them back, asking Taignoagny to come to his ship with Donnacona and Agona.

"It's a trap," said Donnacona that night. "Kart-yeh wants to catch us all."

"He's playing devilish tricks," Taignoagny added. "I just heard that they are leaving the small ship here. So many of his men died there aren't enough to sail it back. Cartier's given it to the Sitadin across the river so they can have the metal and wood."

"Why would he not give that ship to us?" Domagaya was incredulous. "He stayed on our land. We fed him and his men all winter. Neguac saved their lives with her medicine."

"Since the day he put up those poles, we have seen that Kart-yeh is a liar." Contarea shook his head angrily. "I think Cudouagny is angry with us for letting these French live on our land. That is why so many of our people died."

The next day Taignoagny and Domagaya went to see Cartier. The two largest French ships were crawling with sailors at work. They had taken the sails off for the winter, now they were up on the masts and yards, tying them back on.

The brothers wouldn't go on board. Taignoagny called to Cartier from across the water. "Will you take that captive we discussed?"

Cartier shook his head. "No. My king has forbidden me to take any men or women back with us, only the children who have been given to us. They will learn our language and be returned next year."

These words were like the first robin of spring to the brothers. "Then we'll come back tomorrow with our father," Domagaya said.

"I don't trust that dog," Taignoagny hissed as they walked back to their village. "I won't be happy until his ships sail out of sight."

But Donnacona was relieved to hear Cartier's promise. "He is my blood brother," he told his sons. "Friends must trust friends."

"That may be true," Taignoagny said. "But don't go on his ship."

The next afternoon, Donnacona led a group of villagers to visit Cartier and found a surprise awaiting them. The French had put up another cross – inside their fort. Cartier waved happily when he saw them.

"This is a special day for our God," Cartier explained pointing at the cross. "Come in and celebrate with us."

In spite of Cartier's friendly manner, Donnacona was afraid. He edged closer to the fort, but kept one eye on the forest. "He won't come inside," Domagaya told Cartier. "My brother has warned him not to."

Hearing this, Cartier had his men make a small fire in front the draw-bridge and they talked for a while. "This is Holy Cross Day in our country," Cartier said to Donnacona. "Come feast with us and drink wine to honour our God as we have honoured your great Cudouagny."

Whether it was instinct or a finely tuned sense of danger, Taignoagny felt he had to act. He wheeled around to face the villagers who'd come with them. "Run," he yelled. "Get into the trees."

But Cartier had cunningly appealed to Donnacona's spiritual nature. The Iroquois chief dropped his wariness and walked into the fort.

"Seize him," Cartier yelled to his men. Instantly, they grabbed

Donnacona's arms, jamming their guns into his gut.

"Father!" Domagaya cried.

"Get him, too," Cartier yelled to his men. "And him. And him. Grab him, too." Before they could move, Domagaya, Taignoagny, Contarea and another sachem were taken by the sailors. They grabbed their knives and threw them to the ground. The Iroquois villagers howled and yelled from the trees. They didn't dare come out for fear of being shot.

"You dogs," snarled Taignoagny to the sailors. "I knew we should have killed you." One of the sailors smashed him in the face with his gun, knocking him to the sand. Blood poured out his broken nose, blackening the grass.

"You betrayed us," cried Domagaya, "after all we've done for you. You are a liar, Cartier. Your god will be angry with you."

Cartier laughed. "But my king will be very happy."

"Taignoagny! Domagaya! Quiet!" their father commanded. "Remember, you are Iroquois. The Great Spirit will look after us."

The agouhanna of Kanata held his head high as he led the frightened captives to the dark French ships sitting in the river.

EPILOGUE

Donnacona, Domagaya, Taignoagny and seven other Iroquois were taken to France where Donnacona and his sons met King François 1st. Cartier's next voyage to New France was delayed because of the French war with Spain. By the time he left Saint-Malo for New France five years later, in 1541, all but one of the Iroquois, a girl, were dead. Sixty-two years later, when Samuel Champlain travelled up the St. Lawrence in 1603, the people of Kanata and Hochelaga were no longer there. The St. Lawrence Iroquois had disappeared. Whether they died from European diseases, were killed in warfare or simply moved remains a mystery.

Warmed by the fire, Thanadelthur begins her story.

Thanadelthur

*"She was the most remarkable person
that either of us had occasion to meet
in all our worldly travels."*

Ach, I'm glad to see you've finally arrived. Come, sit by our sorry, dwindling fire. I've just thrown on a scrap of driftwood. As you can see, there's little else on this wind-blasted place. But perhaps before you sit, you could find a twig or two, for we are mighty cold. Will you listen to that northern howl? Like the banshee wolves of hell lurking about in the dark, licking the drool from their bloodthirsty lips. In fact, perhaps you could pick up that fresh and glistening bone over there. Aye, that one, and throw it into the black where the yellow eyes are shining. Good. That should appease their toothy cravings for a time. What manner of bone was that? All in good time, my friend. All in good time.

But I'm forgetting my manners. And manners are of a necessity in these forlorn and unremembered parts. My name is William Stuart, formerly in the service of the great and mighty Honourable Company of Gentlemen Adventurers. You know it, I'm certain, by its less heroic name – the Hudson's Bay Company. And lying over there, swaddled in all the ragged furry finery of the north, is none other than Governor James Knight himself, Master of the Company's fort at York. Aye, it's just southward down this briny bay, the busiest fur trading post on the continent. But don't worry, your stirring will not disturb him, for he is seventy-five years old and dead tired, and even this rocky bed of Marble Island is not hard enough to wake him.

I am sorry to say that our hospitality is suffering at the moment, for our cooking pot is empty. Perhaps you would like a swallow or two of tea? Then just reach over and strip a few dry leaves off that bush behind you, and we will melt some snow and make some *thé du bois*, as those French scoundrels call it.

See how Mr. Knight sleeps under that blanket of downy snow. He and I have been tending this peerie fire for some time now, and when we're not nodding off and dreaming of home and hearth, we are swapping stories

Honourable Company of Gentlemen Adventurers
called the "Governor and Company of Adventurers of England tradeing into Hudson's Bay" in its founding charter of 1670, this British company was soon known as the Hudson's Bay Company (HBC).

thé du bois
literally, "tea of the woods"

peerie
small; one of the most-used Orcadian words. In later usage, it became "peedie", as in "peedie-breeks", a little child.

about all the things we've seen and done and loved in our glorious, bedraggled lives. And so, if you have the time and the inclination, I will tell you, as the bard himself would say, a winter's tale that will chill your bones to the quick. She was the most remarkable person that either of us had occasion to meet in all our worldly travels. And now that you are settled and the fire has been stoked, and the tea has chased the north wind from your bones for a while, I will begin. It is the strange and wonderous tale of a slave woman from the Barren Lands.

Her name was Thanadelthur.

It was November, a cruel dark month in these northern latitudes, for winter snows came early that year and piled high against the palisades of York Fort, making every step one of heavy labour. The year was 1714. My God, can seven years have passed so quickly? We had just reclaimed the place with stout Scottish and English lads and taken down the pale froggy flag and hoisted the crisp new British colours. It still flutters proudly over that low, damp place.

Mr. Knight and I were in his quarters before the fire, enjoying a pipe and a thimble of brandy after the rabbit pie that Cookie had served that evening. There was a strange shuffling, a knock at the door, and one of the Company servants barged in. He had with him two of our Home Cree and they were half-dragging, half-carrying something between them. They dropped their ragged cargo by the hearth.

"We were goose hunting, sir, at Ten Shilling Creek, when she came stumbling out of the woods. Fell right at our feet by the tent, she did, mumbling. She's a Copper, sir. But she speaks fair Cree."

Mr. Knight and I exchanged looks of wonderment. Then the scraps of buckskin and fur before us stirred and we put our pipes aside and got down on our knees to unravel the mystery before us. She was young, perhaps fourteen, just barely alive, nothing but skin and bones. But we could see that she had been bonnie once, and would be again perhaps. She had the flat brown face of Copper women, with a broad handsome nose and full wide lips. Her eyes were closed, and as she struggled to open them, doughty old Mr. Knight leaned over and raised her up against himself. Brushing the straggly black hair from her eyes, as if she had been his granddaughter, he raised his glass of amber to her lips.

the bard
a reference to the great English playwright William Shakespeare

Barren Lands
the name the British gave Canada's arctic tundra and taiga regions

York Fort
one of the earliest HBC forts on Hudson Bay. It changed hands several times between the warring English and French from its founding in 1682 until 1714, when the English took control for good. It soon became the company's most important post, and was later known as York Factory.

Home Cree
bands of Cree who, because of a close partnership with the HBC, came to settle in "plantations" or camps outside the walls of Company posts. Those at York Fort soon obtained European weapons, which made them feared by the Dene and others.

Copper
one of the names the English gave to the Eastern Dene, the people of the northern forests in what are now Manitoba and Nunavut

"Drink," he said in Cree, for Mr. Knight spoke a fair bit of it himself. She blinked with her doe-dark eyes, sipped a little and coughed.

Now the orders flew fast and furious. "Go to Cookie. Get hot broth and bread," he said to the hunter. And to the Cree: "Find her warm clothes. Clean, too." As the three hurried away, he turned to me. "Some blankets, William. From the trunk. We must get her out of these cold wet rags."

Inside of half an hour, she was sitting up in front of the fire, huddled in our woolen blankets. Her hands shook as she slurped the broth and in her brown eyes – I'm sure it wasn't the firelight – there was a fierce burning I had never seen before, not in any sane man, not in any woman for certain. When she was sufficiently thawed, she began to speak, and it was a horrible tale she told.

It had begun a year before. With a small group of her Copper people, she was following the caribou south from the Barren Lands when a war party of Cree attacked. The men were killed in the avenging of some old debt, and two young women were carried off as slaves. Their Cree master – Natawapish was his name – took them as his wives and forced them to heavy labour, as is expected of Copper women. But he was a cruel beast. He beat the captives and gave them only scraps of food. Late at night, after the others were asleep, they had to sew moccasins and coats and leggings by the light of the fire, for cold weather was now upon them. And when the Cree moved to their winter grounds, the young women stumbled under the weight of double-heavy loads, so the men could be free to hunt when game appeared.

Despite this hard treatment, she saw that the Cree had wondrous things, traded, she learned, from our fort: guns, knives and cooking pots; blankets like the ones now wrapped around her, needles and fishhooks, as well as thread, combs and other items of great and alluring value.

The two young slaves talked often of escape, but a long year passed. Then this fall, when the Cree were camped on the shore of the Nelson River, the opportunity came. There was a council meeting and while Natawapish was busy attending there, the captives lifted the hem of the tent and crept off into the forest. They circled around to the river, stole a birch canoe and launched it in the frigid water. The night was clear, with a cold breeze from the west. They drifted downstream, hardly daring to

THANADELTHUR'S
LIKELY ROUTE,
NOVEMBER 1714

Hudson Bay

friend's death ✕

turnaround towards camp

toward Dene land

YORK FACTORY ○

GOOSE HUNTING CAMP

Ten Shilling Creek

dragged downstream

Nelson River

Hayes River

Rapids ◎

○

NATAWAPISH'S CAMP

maelstrom
(MAIL-strom) a whirlpool; the original meaning "whirling stream" referred to a whirlpool on the west coast of Norway

breathe, listening for the alarm of dogs and men, but only silence and the west wind followed.

Exhausted, borne by the current, the two lassies fell fast asleep. But the spirits must have been angry, she said, for suddenly they awoke to an awful sound: the roar of white water, the thunder of falls. It was too late. Into the maelstrom they drifted, powerless against the current. They were swept to the brink and over.

In the foaming chaos, they were thrown from the canoe. Pummelled by water, battered by rocks, somehow they survived the boiling cauldron and were finally swept into a quiet pool, first one, then the other. Badly bruised and half-drowned, they staggered ashore and as the sun rose they watched bits and pieces of their canoe float by.

The slave woman coughed and Mr. Knight and I were shaken from our wild reverie. We leaned forward, offered her more broth and some fresh sweet tea that Cookie had brought. She sipped as I poked the fire. The flames and the candles cast hulking shadows upon the rough-sawn walls as she continued.

The two young women decided then that they would go overland to the Barrens to find their people. Hungry and cold, with winter looming, they turned northward. Using the sun by day and the Wolf Star at night, they began their trek. They fought through the gnarly, strangling bush and slogged across the mushy lowlands. They camped on dry gravel hummocks, and ate when their snares found a rabbit or a ptarmigan. But there was little game and the other girl grew faint and often lagged behind. Soon she took sick and could not walk. The slave woman built a fire and a shelter for her friend, then set all the snares, but her traps could find no meat. She herself gnawed the dried red berries still clinging to low bushes, grey caribou lichen from under the snow, and other plants she knew. One cold morning, she awoke to find her friend dead and frozen stiff.

She knew then she would not make it to her northern lands; there was not time. So, after laying her friend out on the ground and singing a song to send her to the spirit land, she turned and angled back. South toward the mighty river, west toward the coast, she headed for the camps of the English she knew lay by the sea. Chased by winter storms that blew in from the north, she dared not stop. And as she walked and stumbled and sometimes even crawled, she longed for the fine things the Cree had, the guns and knives, especially the warm blankets. Finally, past caring if she was awake or dreaming or already dead, she saw tracks and smelled smoke from our goose hunters' fire.

All was silent for a while, save the occasional snapping of the fire, as Mr. Knight and I remained lost in our dark and chilly thoughts. Finally he spoke. "You're safe here, girl. Now go, rest. We have a bed ready for you." He summoned our servants who had been waiting outside. The slave woman stood. She was not much more than five feet tall, and with her eyes half-closed, she was led away, still clutching tightly at her blankets.

With nary a word, Mr. Knight poured us both a soothing bit of brandy. Then he looked at me with a quizzical eye. "I wonder, William, if she did not eat her friend?"

Wolf Star
the North Star

ptarmigan
(TAR-mi-gan): this plump, chicken-like bird summers in the high Arctic and winters on the tundra. Both willow and rock ptarmigan molt their mottled brown feathers and turn white in winter.

dried red berries
kinnikinnick: a member of the heather family used as emergency food because the berries stay on the plant over winter

67

"I wondered that myself," I answered. There was another long pause as we recollected upon the awful strangeness of the story.

"What did she say her name was?"

"I do not know, sir. Come to think upon it, I don't think she ever said."

"She's Copper and speaks passable Cree. She could be of great service to us in our intention."

And so Mr. Knight had her take up residence at the factory where she lived in a tiny room. In a few days, she was rested and eating hearty as a soldier. And soon thereafter, Mr. Knight invited me to sup with him, to hear more of the slave woman's stories, he said. Her health had much improved and her face was filling out again. She had made a pointed caribou skin dress in the manner of her people and looked very much a young lass, full again of life.

Her brown eyes danced as she talked of her people, whom she called Dene. She told of how they fished for trout and char in the rivers, of the many fur animals in Denendeh, their homeland where the spirit flows. And she was almost fierce in the way she allowed that they would dearly love to trade for long guns and blankets and all the wonderful Company goods that she now so thoroughly enjoyed.

Mr. Knight nodded patiently. "And tell us, is there any yellow metal in your land? Like this?" He held out a pudgy hand and showed her the Company ring embossed with his personal seal.

"Oh yes," she said. "There are rivers and streams where there is shining yellow metal, some of it like scales of fish, some bigger like stones. We make these stones into things such as this." She pulled at a cord around her neck. At its end hung a gleaming amulet that had been hidden inside her dress. I reached for it, a bit hungrily perhaps. It was gold, to be sure, and beautifully shaped. Mr. Knight's eyes brightened at the sight of it, but it was the warmth of it that made me ache.

And so, after a long evening of talk in both Cree and the woman's new halting words of English, she rose to leave. I stopped her as she headed for the door.

"I am sorry to say it, lass, but we do not know your name."

"Thanadelthur," she answered. "Than-a-DELL-thur." She repeated it slowly for our slow white ears.

"What does it mean?" Mr. Knight inquired.

"Marten shake," she said. "When the marten is about to fight, it is very fierce, its whole body shakes." She wheeled

Dene
(DEN-nay): known by the Cree as Chipewyan, "people of the pointy coats", these Athapaskan-speaking people have lived along North America's northern treeline for thousands of years

Denendeh
literally, "the creator's spirit flows through the land"

marten
a fur-bearing carnivor, like a large weasel, that lives and hunts in Canada's northern forests

around to leave then stopped, turned, and with a twinkle in her eye added: "Also when it is ready to mate." She disappeared through the door.

We sat there, tilting back in our post-built chairs, smiling around the stems of our pipes, heads encircled by wreaths of smoke. A remarkable girl, we agreed. A most remarkable girl.

Mr. Knight leaned forward to stir the fire. "I have been forming a plan, William. Would you care to hear it?"

"Aye, sir. That I would."

His strategy was this: we would use this slave woman – he could never wrap his English tongue around her name – to fashion a treaty between the northern Copper and the southern Cree, so that the Copper could safely bring their rich furs down to the bay. To make the trip easier for the Copper people, the Company would build a new trading post farther north along the bay, at the mouth of the Churchill River, where our men had already found an excellent site. In this way, he said, we could expand our enterprise and our westward reach from this great bay on which we were so tentatively perched .

"It's a grand scheme," said Mr. Knight, "but much depends on whether she will lead a party of Cree to her people, so they can stop all this useless fighting and make peace."

When Thanadelthur heard this plan, her eyes lit up. "I am to go home!" she said.

And she immediately began plotting with Mr. Knight for this expedition into what for us was unknown land, *terra incognita*.

"You must make a feast," she said. "For your Home Cree. You must make them believe that peace will be better for them. You must give them many gifts." And she outlined ways in which this could be done.

"And you must give me gifts for my people," she went on. "Things we can carry. We must show them all they can get for their furs." Then she stopped and creased her brow in a frown, perhaps thinking of the long and arduous journey ahead. "What English will you send with us?"

Mr. Knight had already considered that question. Without hesitation, he looked at me. "My servant, William Stuart, will accompany you." There was a slight upward movement at the corners of her mouth as she nodded, then

diplomacy
the art of international relations, as in negotiating alliances or treaties between two hostile groups

servant
the term the HBC used for all its junior or lower-ranked employees

turned and left the room. I felt my heart beating hard, likely in anticipation of the daunting adventure. But also, perhaps, because I would be in the pro-longed company of the lovely Thanadelthur.

Preparations went ahead. I learned what I could of her Copper tongue; she learned what she could of the King's English. One day we were dis-cussing how we'd travel. "I think because we're going far inland," I said, "we should take canoes up the Hayes, to the uplands, then travel north on foot from there."

No! "No!" She shook her head wildly, her face full of fear. "That is where the Cree are! And Natawapish!" She shuddered, then set her jaw. "We will walk. It is the Dene way."

Mr. Knight heard of this later. "Well, at least we'll use the bloody sloop to ferry you across the Nelson. No use starting out with wet feet. They'll be soaking soon enough."

Spring came, then a bonny June and a great feast was held just outside the palisade. The banks of the river were littered with canoes as word spread among the Cree. The ground was dotted with fires. Women turned spits of green spruce bent with the weight of roasting moose and venison. Under tri-pods erected over other fires, geese, ducks and ptarmigan swung from cords, sizzling, dripping with fat as they slowly spun. The drums beat night and day, as everyone from grandmothers to tiny children sang and danced and ate.

As the Cree are fond of speeches, Mr. Knight gave a long and eloquent address. So did Wapasu, the Cree captain, who would lead his people on this long peace march. Thanadelthur was introduced as our interpreter and Mr. Knight took great care to show his affection for her. He announced that she would be under my protection and expressed his grave desire that no harm should come to her. After that, the gifts were handed out. During this time, several bands of upland Cree arrived at the post laden with winter furs and they, too, were pressed upon to join the expedition.

And so it was that on the sunny morning of the 27th day of June, 1715, we left the fort. Cannons boomed and guns were fired from the ramparts. The remaining Cree waved and cried and shouted their well wishes. We were 150 strong, more men than women, and a dozen or more dogs for pulling loads in winter, or for eating if it came to that. We walked Indian file,

sloop
a single-masted boat with a single sail, used by the HBC for ferrying goods and people along the shore of Hudson Bay

palisade
a fence of poles (or pales) forming a fortification

venison
the meat of deer or caribou

Wapasu, Thanadelthur and I in the lead. We headed west along the Hayes, past the crumbling French chapel, past a deer hedge where the Cree trapped game. By afternoon, we reached an ancient path that travelled northward across the peninsula. It was an eight-mile trip and the evening star was out when we reached the Nelson and pitched our tents.

muskeg
(MUS-keg) from the Cree *maskeek*, a swamp or bog formed by accumulating moss, leaves and decayed matter

The company sloop was there next morning, just as Mr. Knight had promised. The captain and a crew of two had sailed around the headland and up the river, still wide and sluggish at that point. We loaded our supplies, women, men and an assortment of half-wild, barking dogs. Trip after trip, we rowed the sloop across, our long oars flashing in the sun. We landed on a point, just north of a small island on the northern shore, then began to walk.

unguent
a soothing salve or ointment

Very soon, we came across a small river emptying from the north. Turning to leave the Nelson behind – I would not see it for almost a year – we worked our way northward up the stream. For a week we travelled along the ragged shore, rising before the sun, stopping late to camp on the river-bank. Our Cree carriers lugged the heavy packs of supplies and gifts, men and women straining forward with straps of skin across their foreheads. The women often carried the biggest loads. Even the dogs dragged tent poles as we walked northward.

kinnikinnic
also called bearberry or upland cranberry, this ground trailing shrub grows across the north and Arctic and keeps its leaves year round. The berries are rather taste-less raw, but better when cooked and, with the leaves, are good for tea. The dried leaves were also used as a sub-stitute for tobacco.

The land around the bay was flat and low, thick with brush, stunted trees, and great watery swaths of bog. The muskeg sucked at our feet with every step. We meandered like a buckskin snake, always searching for dry ground. Yet dry ground was choked with tangled willow, tamarack and spruce that we were forced to slip under, step over or walk around.

On the Nelson or at the fort, the stiff bay breeze had often kept the mosquitoes, black flies and deer flies at bay. But out on the land, the shining ponds were breeding grounds for millions of the pesky beasts, and they nearly drove us mad. With every step, black clouds of bugs swarmed up and attacked. Thanadelthur and the Cree were used to this. They had smeared bear grease on their exposed skin, even their eyes and ears and noses, to discourage the voracious creatures. But I had turned up my nose at their disagreeable unguent and soon my eyes were nearly swollen shut and my shirt was a bloody mass of red.

That night, in our tent – for Mr. Knight had dictated that we should share a tent to prevent any ill-conceived designs – Thanadelthur made medicine for my wounds. She picked small oval leaves, called kinnikinnic leaves, chopped them with the plant's red berries and boiled them for a while. First, she gave me some to drink and it made a refreshing tea. When the solution cooled, she dipped a scrap of cloth into it and carefully swabbed my bites. In a short while the pain had lessened. I was much impressed with her gentle care. "Thank you very much," I said.

"The Great Spirit guides everything we do", she murmured. "It is the Creator who needs to be thanked." She threw grass and green branches onto the fire, making a smudge that drove the mosquitoes and blackflies from our tent. Then she lay down across from me and I drifted off to sleep after a brief prayer of thanks to my own uncertain god.

Before long, auguries of trouble appeared. Thanadelthur had pitched into our labours with a will, walking swiftly at the front. "My heart is singing," she said to me one day. "I am on the land again and I am going home." But two of the upland Cree assigned to be our carriers were surly, sullen fellows. They had heard of the slave woman and knew of her escape. They resented Thanadelthur's esteemed position in our party.

"Walk faster," she said to them one day after noticing their loafing efforts. "Do you need a Dene woman to show you how?" They muttered darkly and quickened their steps for a while, but soon lapsed into their indifferent pace at the tail end of our column.

As we continued north and westward, the land rose slightly; the uplands it was called. The trees grew taller here, the forests thickened, and here and there were fields of jumbled, glistening rock. We were getting low on food and a hunting party went out, but there were no caribou to be found and our hunters came back disappointed and angry.

"It's the fault of that Chipewyan woman," they said, for that was their name for the Copper people. "She must be menstruating; she must have allowed our hunters to cross her path. Her power has brought us bad luck."

Thanadelthur was furious. "It is not my time you fools." She spat at the feet of the hunters. "You cowardly Cree can only make a kill when your quarry is sleeping, like my people when you attacked and killed them. You are dogs that you would blame your failure on me." And she stomped off.

That night the Cree made offerings of tobacco to the spirits of the deer and the next day, they shot six, as well as several ducks. One hundred and fifty mouths feasted hungrily, the trouble forgotten for the moment. Once the little bit of surplus meat and some fish had been smoked, we packed again to resume our journey.

Before long, we reached a peerie river. As it was noon, we stopped to eat.

Chipewyan
a Cree word for the Dene, their northern neighbours, with whom they were on hostile terms in the early eighteenth century. It means "pointy skins", and was likely a reference to the design of their anoraks or outer coats, which were long front and back, and cut high on the sides.

Curlew. Curlew.

The women unwrapped their gill nets of twine and cast them into the water, fastening them with sticks pushed into the mud. Then the men threw off their shirts, though the women kept theirs on, and everyone ran into the water, splashing each other and swimming.

"Are you not coming in?" Wapasu's wife, Sissipuk cried to me.

"I cannot swim," I answered in ruddy-faced embarrassment. The waters of my boyhood in Orkney had always been too cold to learn.

"You are a shore bird. A curlew." She laughed and soon the others joined in with a chorus: "Curlew. Curlew."

I dismissed their teasing with a wave, got up to walk along the shore and find a quiet place to write my journal. Upstream, around the bend, something glittered in the pebbled river bottom. I knelt on a rock to see what it was.

"What are you looking at?" Thanadelthur appeared behind me, barefoot, dripping in her caribou skin.

"I thought I saw something shining," I said.

She paused for a moment. "Was it the yellow metal?"

I nodded. "Perhaps. Will you show me the rivers where it's found when we get to your country?"

No answer. I turned to look at her. Too late. She pushed me and I toppled in, clothes and all.

I came up, spluttering, laughing, expecting Thanadelthur to be laughing, too. "What is so important about yellow metal?" She was standing, hands on her hips, angry as a hissing goose. "I don't like the hungry look I see when you talk about that metal." She turned and strode quickly back to the others.

After lunch, we waded across the river, and keeping the sun behind us and to the left, we walked northward. Thanadelthur stayed away from me that day, and that night she froze me out with silence as she cooked. I sat watching, slapping mosquitoes, as she cut up a fish caught at noon and threw it whole – head, guts, scales and all – into the iron pot that she set into the fire to boil. She must have seen the look on my face. "If you don't like the food I cook, you can starve," she snarled.

"No ... no," I stammered. "It's just that, in my country, we remove the innards before we cook it. The scales, too. We slice them off."

"How wasteful your women are," she replied. I got up, having lost my appetite, and retreated to Wapasu's and Sissipuk's fire. The Cree had splayed their fish on sticks, angled them over the fire and were roasting them slowly.

curlew
considered now to be nearly extinct, Eskimo curlews, a long-legged shorebird of the far north, were once so abundant they darkened the skies during migration. Among the world's fastest fliers, they had no fear of most predators and so were easy prey for men with guns.

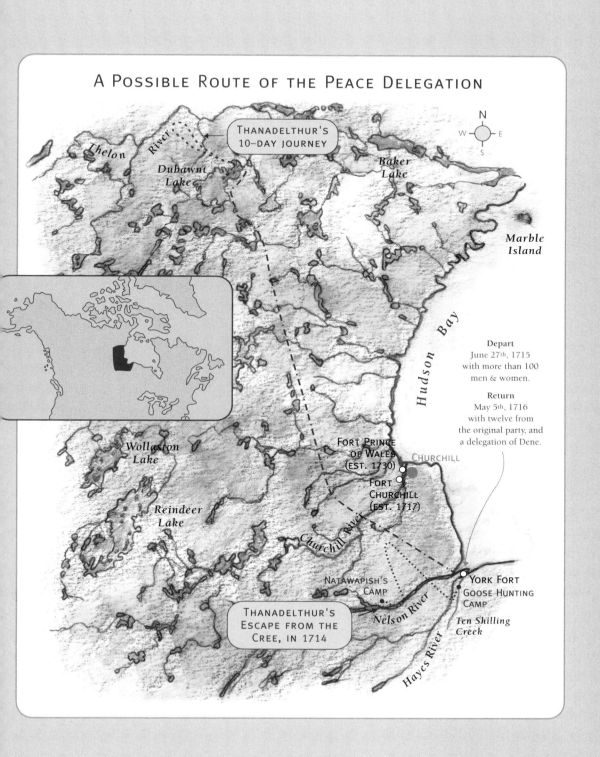

A POSSIBLE ROUTE OF THE PEACE DELEGATION

Thelon

Dubawnt Lake

River

THANADELTHUR'S 10–DAY JOURNEY

Baker Lake

Marble Island

Hudson Bay

Wollaston Lake

Reindeer Lake

FORT PRINCE OF WALES (EST. 1730)

CHURCHILL

FORT CHURCHILL (EST. 1717)

Churchill River

Depart
June 27th, 1715
with more than 100
men & women.

Return
May 5th, 1716
with twelve from
the original party, and
a delegation of Dene.

THANADELTHUR'S ESCAPE FROM THE CREE, IN 1714

NATAWAPISH'S CAMP

Nelson River

YORK FORT
GOOSE HUNTING CAMP

Ten Shilling Creek

Hayes River

Without a word, Sissipuk handed me a piece. Wapasu grunted, licked his fingers and kept on eating.

The next morning our scouts brought back news. There was a wide river and a series of lakes ahead. They could find no way around. And no signs of friendly tribes who might ferry us over. We would have to raft across. When we reached the shore, the Cree were already at work chopping the taller spruce that grew near the water. Everyone joined in. Chips flew as iron axes bit into the wood. They, like the iron knives, were gifts from Mr. Knight. I helped by lopping off the branches. The women dragged each log into the water and tied them together with babiche, strips of hide stored in bags for needs such as this. By evening we were done, eleven rafts made and ready.

"We cross tomorrow morning?" I asked Wapasu.

He looked at the sky. "There will be a strong wind tomorrow," he said, pointing east. "With rain. We will go tonight when it is dark."

I looked up at the sky, but saw only wispy streaks of mare's tails. "Why wait until dark?" I asked. "Isn't that dangerous?"

"It would be dangerous if a war party was watching from the other side and we were sitting on rafts. They could play Shoot The Squirrel until we were dead." He laughed at my discomfort.

That night, as we waited in the trees, the wind came earlier than Wapasu had predicted. We tied the rafts to the trees, and set up our tents to wait. For three days the wind blew, soaking us with a fine cold rain from low grey clouds. We sat in our tents and watched as whitecaps chased each other down the lake.

"The lake spirit is unhappy," said Thanadelthur on the second evening.

"Why?" I asked, looking up from my notebook where I was working on a map of our journey.

She shrugged. "What are those pictures you are making?"

"It is a map, to show where we have come on our walk."

"What is this line that looks like a snake?"

"That's the Nelson River where we crossed. See, this is where we followed that smaller river. And this is where we got the deer."

"You are not good at making pictures," she said. "A child could draw better than that."

"Yes," I admitted, smiling. "But they're not real pictures. They're a special way of drawing so others coming after us can know how we got here."

"Other English?" she asked, raising her eyebrows.

I nodded. "Perhaps."

babiche
long strips of hide used for binding things together. They stretch when wet, then shrink as they dry, creating a very tight binding.

"Or maybe those murdering Cree," she said. "That is why the lake spirits are angry. They don't want English or Cree to follow us to our land."

I laughed, and just as quickly stopped.

Wapasu came by our tent the next morning. "Some people have gone," he told me.

I poked my head out. It was still raining. "How many?"

Wapasu stood tall against the grey sky, soaked but showing no signs of being cold. "Fifteen. Those two who carried your packs and their families."

"We'll manage." I didn't know what else to say.

"We will cross tonight if the wind stays down." He turned and walked away. Thanadelthur said nothing but hummed a haunting song as she rose. She opened her little fire bag, decorated with porcupine quills and dyed moose hair, took out a flint, another stone and some dry moss. In a minute, she had a small fire in our tent, the smoke rising out the hole above. She heated the remaining fish soup. When it was hot, we dipped our bowls in and ate without a word.

There was just a breeze that night so we rafted across, our armed scouts in the lead. Halfway across, the rain stopped, the clouds thinned and we could see a half moon behind them. We paddled as silently as we could while the women held the dogs' mouths shut. The scouts landed first; the rest of us waited, the water slapping against our rafts. We were soaked and cold. A grey owl hooted. It was the signal Wapasu was waiting for. He motioned for us to paddle ashore. As we approached, the scouts waded into the water with a warning. They had smelled smoke, but could see no fires. We pulled the rafts in, and while the warriors stood guard, the women quietly unloaded our supplies.

The clouds were thinner now and from time to time the moon broke through. "We cannot stay," Wapasu whispered. "There are bad spirits at this place."

We started walking, away from the trees huddled by the river, and soon were out on open land. The rock glowed like pewter in the moonlight, with drifts of mist settled in the muskeg patches, all eerie greys and black. Silently, we walked. We didn't stop until the morning sun rose high and burned off the fog. Wapasu was still uneasy so we made no fires, chewing dried venison and fish instead. The land was silent. We had not seen a rabbit, not even a plover or a snipe. Thanadelthur pointed up. Overhead, two ravens circled, grim, sharp shapes against the light grey sky. "Those cowardly Cree are grumbling," she said. "More people want to leave."

I don't blame them, I thought, gazing out across the desolate vista. A light wind rose again, this time from the north, and I shivered, perhaps from cold, perhaps from fear.

T he trees were smaller now, the forests thinner. We travelled on strange gravel hills that rose in undulating lines, as if left there by some giant hoe. We angled across the land, winding past ponds where black ducks swam, toward a blue smudge of hills in the distance.

The wind picked up, carrying with it a bitter cold. Thanadelthur did not seem to mind. Her anger toward me had boiled off and she chatted quite

The many wetlands and bogs of Canada's north make survival and travel difficult, unless you're a duck. Most plants and animals prefer drier ridges.

merrily as we strode along. By late afternoon, we arrived at the base of the low mountain of rock. A stream tumbled off the face of it.

"We will camp here," Wapasu said. He motioned to Thanadelthur and me. "Come. We will climb up and look about. It will help us choose our path."

The hill was no higher than those of Hoy, which I had climbed as a boy. I remembered my family as we picked our way up, crossing the stream several times. I was surprised how little I thought of them, how foreign the comforts of a crofter's hearth seemed here in the Nor'Wast. We reached the top and there, cradled by rocks, was a small rainwater lake, the source of our stream.

"Look!" Thanadelthur said excitedly, pointing west. The sun was low and before it on the horizon stretched a long, silvery gash in the darkening land. It was a lake, shining to the south. "Soon we will see another lake, so big we cannot look across it," she said, pleased to spot a familiar landscape.

Wapasu looked north and westward. "There is a river that way," he said, pointing at a darker line of green. "We will find animals there. We are low on food and need to hunt and fish." The sun was setting now, smearing the wet grey clouds with angry red. We walked to the edge of the little lake, thick with cattails and wiry willows.

"We should gather firewood," said Thanadelthur, and then stopped. I saw the expression on her face, turned to the water and saw something floating, just beneath the surface. It was a wolf; its white belly bloated, the face half eaten. I thought of the people down below making soup and tea.

Wapasu walked ahead around the shore. He stopped, kicked at something half in the water. Another wolf. Our Cree captain stared across the pool. "Witches have poisoned the water." He turned and flashed a look at Thanadelthur. "Come," he said. "Let's leave this place." But before we left, he sprinkled tobacco on the pond and said a short prayer.

The Cree had pitched their teepees beside the pleasant stream. Most had already eaten and were sitting by small fires. Some men greased their guns and sharpened knives and arrowheads. The women sewed new moccasins or repaired old ones torn by the rough travel. Thanadelthur and I pitched our tent in silence.

When we were done, she picked up our iron pot to get water from the stream. I grabbed her hand. "Don't."

"Why?" Her eyes squinted with the question.

"The water," I motioned to the hill. "I am afraid it is not good."

"But the others have already eaten and made their tea."

"I know. It was too late to warn them."

We were both tired, tired of the rough travel and the never-ending possibility of danger, tired of sleeping on rocky ground, tired of the cold and rain. Worse, it would soon be getting colder. We crawled wearily into our tent and ate the last bits of smoked fish and tough, dry venison. We placed our sleeping blankets on either side of the fire, our feet pointing toward the door. The way we always did.

Nor'Wast
literally, the North West, a name for the nothern reaches of North America, which would one day become Canada.

79

"Tell me a story," Thanadelthur said as we lay in the dark. "Tell me about your country, about your houses and your women."

"It's a green and rolling land," I began, feeling drowsy yet happy to oblige. "With many small islands in a great ocean." I stretched my arms to show her the expanse of sea and promptly fell asleep. Perhaps I was dreaming, but I thought she touched my hand.

"Witch!"

Thunk. Something hard hit the walls of our tent.

"Sorceress!" A woman yelled.

Thunk. Thunk. A scream. I shot up.

"What is it? Are you hurt?" Thanadelthur was sitting up, shaking.

I peeked outside. Twenty Cree stood in front of our tent. A woman launched another rock. Thunk.

 "Stop!" I pulled on my breeches, opened the flap and stumbled barefoot into the morning light. "What is it?"

"She has poisoned us!" a woman yelled. "My husband is sick and dying."

"Everyone is sick," a Cree warrior said. "She has cast a spell on us."

"Is this true? Are people sick?" I looked around. "Where is Wapasu?"

"Hunting," said a warrior, his spear poised and ready.

"Give that Chipewyan witch to us. We must drive her out."

I raised my hand. "Quiet! Please!" The shouting stopped. "Tell me, how many are sickly? How are they suffering?"

"My husband threw up all his food," said one woman. "He could not make it outside. He messed himself."

"My wife lies moaning in our tent," a man shouted. "She has an evil fire inside her. The fever is on her face."

I held my hand up again. "Listen to me, friends. It is the water in the stream that made you ill. We saw dead wolves in the water at the top of the mountain yesterday. That's where the stream comes from. It is the water, not Thanadelthur, that made your people sick."

"What magic is it that you are not sick?" a warrior asked.

There was a noise behind me. "We did not drink the water," Thanadelthur answered, standing up beside me, her eyes flashing fire. "Wapasu was there. Did he not tell you? And why are you not sick? And you? And you?" she asked, pointing at her accusers.

They muttered to each other.

"You Cree are so quick to blame. Like mangy dogs, you come barking at my tent." She stormed off, angrily ripped at a nearby bush and returned with a handful of grey-green soapberry leaves. "Pick these," she said. "Send the men to find good water away from here. Make medicine with this and give it to the sick. If the spirits aren't angry because you are such sorry stupid people, they might let you live."

It was a black day. The Cree retched and moaned and ran stumbling into the bushes. Their tents reeked of sickness. Another stream was found, not far away, and many carried water to the camp while others searched the bushes for leaves. Wapasu and his hunters came back grim and empty-handed; grimmer still when they heard the news. We stayed another day, then two more. Thanadelthur was fair restless.

"Let's leave the sick behind," she said to Wapasu one day. "They can catch up when they're better."

Wapasu, who was taller by a head, looked down at her. "They will not follow if we leave them now. They'll go home."

"Good," she said coldly. "Let them go. Winter will be here soon enough and we have far to travel."

Wapasu's dark, lined face was stern. The burden of responsibility lay heavily across his buckskin shoulders and I sensed that he was squirming in this marten trap. "I will talk with the others," he said.

The next morning we took our leave; a sorrowful parting for the Cree, a relief for Thanadelthur. As we prepared to go, the Cree women touched each other on the cheeks, then hoisted their packs onto their backs, tied tent poles and small packs to the dogs and bending forward, fell into the line of moving men. We left thirty people behind, some still very sick, but others feeling better and out of danger.

We walked north for two days toward the river that Wapasu had seen from the mountain. The river flowed from a long, narrow lake that the scouts said we did not need to cross, but could go around at the far end. Here larger trees skirted the water and we saw signs of deer and moose.

soapberry
also widely known as buffalo berry, this bush has small elongated oval leaves that are silvery on the undersides. It bears bright red berries that are bitter when raw but delicious in jelly or cooked. Some native peoples beat the berries with water to make a whipped foam. Farther south, plains people cooked the berries with buffalo roasts.

A barren-ground caribou bull, resplendent in velvet-covered antlers, pauses in his summer migration. His journey might take him hundreds of miles between March and October.

Quickly, we set up camp, happy to have good water again. That evening the hunters brought back three caribou and the next day four more. The women had been fishing, too, and gathering wild raspberries in their birch containers. Wapasu ordered that the meat be cut and smoked as quickly as possible. A party of four women and six warriors volunteered to take fresh food and water back to the sick Cree and their families camped at the evil mountain.

We waited, but no one was ever idle. After supper the women sewed and patched. One day, Thanadelthur pulled out a caribou skin she'd been using as a sleeping mat. She flipped it over, fur side down and began marking it with a blackened stick from the fire.

"What are you doing?" I asked. I had cleaned and oiled my gun, which I had yet to fire on this journey.

"I am making winter moccasins for us," she said. "We will need them soon." She finished sketching four T-shaped patterns on the hide, then with her knife carefully cut them out. She pulled a thick new needle from her babiche bag and started sewing with thin cords of gut.

"Why not use the Company thread?" I asked.

"It is not strong enough," she said. "It is fine for beads and shirts but not for this. Walking is hard on thread."

"It's hard on feet, too." Her eyes crinkled at my poor joke.

Each piece she'd cut became a single moccasin and legging combined that would reach up almost to our knees, with the seams running along the top and front. Thanadelthur's hands flitted like birds as she sewed, using a small piece of wood to push the needle through, then tugging each loop tight. "These will keep the snow and water out," she said, smiling shyly, suddenly embarrassed at being watched. "Does your woman sew?" she asked as she studied her work.

"I don't have a woman and you know it." I laughed. "I'm just a poor Company servant and it's not allowed. Perhaps when I get back to Orkney." My voice trailed off. That I might actually go home some day seemed like a dream, far beyond the horizon. Thanadelthur knotted the sewing cord, cut it with her knife, then turned the piece so that the fur was on the outside. "Here," she said, handing one to me. "Try it."

I pulled it on. I didn't know what to say. "I believe it's a mite too big," I said, wiggling my foot around.

"No," she laughed. "I will make other moccasins for inside, otherwise your feet would freeze."

wild raspberries
delicious berries that grow in woodland clearings and on south-facing slopes. They are found from British Columbia to Newfoundland and north to Nunavut.

gut
the intestines of some animals prepared for use as strings for sewing or for sutures

83

"Will it be that cold?" A silver shiver ran down my neck.

"Yes," she said, suddenly serious. "It will be that cold."

The food party returned in three days; their light loads had meant fast travel. Quickly we packed our tents and the fresh-smoked fish and meat. Following the river north, we skirted a small lake, then angled north-west. We waded across a small river, then came across a bigger one where we built rafts and prepared again to cross at night. But the September moon was full and we waited for it to set, so it would be dark when we crossed. The nights were cool now. There was mist on the water and it helped to hide us as we paddled.

Game was scarce. There were few signs of life and before long we were low on food again. But we pressed on, pushing, always pushing. We waded across another cold river, and then, before we could dry out again, another. And in between, as always, muskeg and rock and trees growing smaller and smaller.

land of little sticks
the Dene name for the transitional forest that separates Canada's boreal forests from its tundra region

lichen
several kinds of plants consisting of a fungus that grows with certain algae. They form a crust-like growth on rocks and trees and provide necessary food for caribou.

disdain
an attitude of contempt or scorn

The landscape was flat and bleak as if some great knife had scraped it, but strewn with vast fields of jumbled boulders. Huge mottled patches of grey-green lichen grew ankle deep and crunched beneath our feet. Every low spot was filled with black, brackish water, often frozen now in the morning, surrounded by small bushes and reeds. Willows and birch grew short in shaggy clumps. One day Wapasu and I stood beside a stunted tamarack, about his height.

"How old do you think this tree is?" he asked.

"I don't know, five years, maybe six."

"Maybe 200 years old," he said and laughed. "The sun is not warm here for long in summer."

"My people call this the land of little sticks," Thanadelthur said as she came up beside us.

"It is a barren place," I said.

Thanadelthur furrowed her brow. "What is this word, 'barren'?"

"It means empty, without life."

She looked at me, her eyes flashed with anger, if not outright disdain. Just then, in the distance, a ptarmigan flew up, an explosion of white and brown. "You English," she said, shaking her head. Like an angry marten.

One clear night there was a ring around the pallid moon. The air was still and cold. And next morning the ponds were frozen solid. "Before long, the caribou will come," said Thanadelthur, her happiness restored again. "They come south for winter food, and behind them will be my people."

A few days later, a chill wind blew into our teeth as we crossed a small river. The soaring white clouds of summer were gone. Every day, dark, brooding lumps hurled themselves across the autumn sky. The summer greens were gone, too, as low bushes and trees turned scarlet and bright yellow. The lichen dried and crunched under foot. And morning and evening, we heard the haunting chatter of geese as they gathered, preparing for their journey south. I envied them their wings. Fearful of spending winter in this formidable land, I longed to join their leaving.

"We will stop here to make snowshoes," Wapasu said as we came across a small round pond ringed by tall black spruce. "There is good wood here and it will snow soon. Perhaps tonight."

As we put up our tents, a loon called out, a lonely tremolo. I had grown to love that song, yet found it disturbing, too, and sad. I waited for an answering cry. There was none. Thanadelthur had been watching me. She stopped adjusting the wood tent pole. "That loon will die here," she said.

"How in Heaven's name, lass, can you know that?"

"The pond is too small. It landed here because it was tired, but the loon is a heavy bird and needs more water than there is here to take flight." She paused. "Look up. You might see its mate still flying around."

I could see no other loon, but an awful picture formed in my mind: large flakes of snow sifting down, the solitary loon paddling around, grown hoarse from calling, its mournful mate long gone, swimming in ever smaller circles as ice closed in on the dark water. Does it know what lies ahead? I wondered. Do I?

I slept fitfully that night. In dreams, wolves howled and their howling shook the tent. They circled in, sharp teeth dripping with foaming gore; they tore the hides off our tent poles, then came for us. I sat up with a start. A storm was raging. I had thrown off my furry blankets. Thanadelthur murmured in her sleep. In spite of my shivering, I peeked outside, and got a black slap in the face with stinging snow.

pallid
pale or lacking colour

tremolo
(TREM-a-low) a tremulous or wavering sound caused by the rapid repitition of one or more notes.

The storm still raged in the morning. We stayed long in bed, then Thanadelthur made a fire and we boiled some scraps of deer meat. When that was done I reached outside and scooped up baskets full of snow, which we melted for tea. But the greasy potion did nothing to restore my mood.

We needed wood for the fire and for snowshoes. I dressed, now in the double skin coats and leggings that we had carried along. I put on a fur cap, and moosehide mitts that I had traded with Sissipuk for a knife. The mitts extended well up my arm. She had decorated them with porcupine quills, moose hair, and glass beads from the post. Thanadelthur's mitts were almost without adornment. "My people don't waste time making things so fancy," she sniffed. But she smiled when I admired again the new long moccasins she'd made for me as I slipped them on.

Wâciyê
a greeting in Spoken Cree; it can mean either "hello" or "goodbye"

bairn
a Scottish and Orcadian term for a baby

Snow had piled up again against the tent flap. I pushed it away and crawled outside, into a roaring new world. There was snow everywhere. It blanketed the frozen ground and piled high against the shaking, billowing tents. Drifts buried bushes in macabre shapes. Snow spattered against the sides of trees, turning them into ghosts of gray. Hurtling snow filled the air, filled every stinging inhalation. I winced from the pain of it, wheeled away to suck in a freezing breath. And then I heard it.

A cry in the wind. An infinitesimal bleat.

It cannot be, I thought. No, it is impossible. Like a furry apparition, Thanadelthur rose beside me. I held up a hand. "Listen."

Thanadelthur stopped and threw off her hood. The sound came again. "Come," she said trudging through the knee-deep snow to Wapasu's and Sissipuk's tent. "*Wâciyê!*," she called out in Cree. "Are you all right?"

There was no answer. Then, "Sissipuk has born a child." It was Wapasu. The flap did not move. "She is fine."

A bairn. I was struck dumb. In all these months, I had seen no sign of it.

Thanadelthur leaned close to me and shouted against the wind. "Wood." She pointed to the trees.

Later, in our tent, we carved spruce branches into snowshoe pieces, feeding the whittled scraps into the smouldering fire, stopping often to warm our hands. A pot of meltwater warmed, too, while the wind roared and whistled.

"How can that baby survive?" I asked in horror at the thought. Thanadelthur laughed.

"Do you think every baby is born in summer?" She shrugged. "The Great Spirit looks after babies."

"But Sissipuk, she won't be able to walk for a while, or carry anything."

Thanadelthur laughed again. "Some day I would like to visit your land. I want to see these women of yours. You treat them like little children."

We spent the day carving, Thanadelthur directing every step. After we had squared four long sticks, we held them over the iron pot and poured hot water over them, then bent them slowly, carefully across our knees. We did that until we had four curved pieces. Then I used my small wood awl and drilled holes at both ends. Thanadelthur tied two curved pieces together

awl
a tool for boring holes in wood

A solitary tipi reflects the green glow of the northern lights and the golden radiance of the rising moon.

at the ends with babiche, then wedged two smaller straight sticks between them, forcing them apart until we had the snowshoe shape. "See," she said. "My grandmother taught me this, just as her grandmother taught her."

I drilled more holes along the length. "Tomorrow, I will make the webbing," Thanadelthur said. "Now I am tired." There was no more food. We drank tea but it did nothing to restore us and as we went to sleep that night, our stomachs growled, as if in answer to the howling wind.

The storm continued the next day, just as vicious, its icy teeth sinking into us as we huddled in our tent with no food to warm us. We had tea again for breakfast over a small fire and Thanadelthur had begun to weave the snowshoe webbing when Wapasu came by.

"The storm spirit will be tired by tonight," he said. Sissipuk was fine and so was the baby girl, although they, too, had run out of food. It was still too windy to hunt. I went out later to find more wood. The Cree tents, like our own, were half-buried, almost invisible in this whirling white world. The only sign of human life was when, from time to time, grey shapes ran out, crouched quickly behind a bush, a rock – a futile gesture, I discovered – to relieve themselves, then scampered back to their snowy dens.

That night I marvelled again at Wapasu's abilities, for the wind did die down, the clouds passed and the sky was clear and sparkling cold. And for a second night I went to bed empty, my stomach now in painful knots. Thanadelthur returned from a short nature trip and reached across the dwindling fire.

"Here, chew this."

Ach! "Ach! Are you trying to poison me, lass?" It was sticky, with a sharp, bitter taste."

"It's sap, from the spruce tree. Suck on it. It will stay soft and you can chew it for hours. It is an old Dene trick to cut the hunger."

We broke camp in brilliant sunshine, ravenous, eager to move and find game. All the Cree were hungry, too. Sissipuk, her baby girl wrapped inside her coat, put on her snowshoes, staggered as she swung on her pack, then straightened and joined the march. Wapasu, the Cree and I took turns breaking trail. It was hard work in the deep snow. The Cree snowshoes were longer and narrower than the ones Thanadelthur and I had made. "To go between the trees," she explained. "In their land they grow closer together."

Several of the Cree had made sleds as well as snowshoes. Now they loaded them with packs and tied their dogs in harness made of moose and caribou. The dogs yelped and jumped, tangling the lines and straining against the loads until finally, they were allowed to run.

The world was a sparkling wonder, a great rumpled snowy blanket studded with ribbons of green spruce and bristles of tamarack. The glitter, however, was dangerous so we wrapped flat strips of skin around our heads with little slits for our eyes, to prevent snow blindness. And always, amid all the terrible beauty, there hovered over us and within, the gnawing spectre – hunger. There was no game, not even any sign of game.

Our ragged, dishevelled column now moved northward at a slow pace, slogging through deep snow, with vitality enough to lift one snowshoe, then the other, and little more. The hunters had been gone since before sunrise. Late in the afternoon, they returned. We could see from the way they moved that their outing had been in vain. "I do not feel the hunting spirit with us," Wapasu confided to me as we paused.

That night our Cree captain built an outside fire under the twinkling sky and all the hunters gathered. He banged his drum and they sang songs to the spirit of the caribou, their prayers rising on puffs of steam into the cold night air to mingle with the stars. They asked the caribou to offer themselves to the hunters and their people. In exchange, Wapasu sprinkled a gift of tobacco on the fire. Then we went to bed.

It was cold and bright again the next day and still we saw no game. "Sometimes," said Thanadelthur as we walked, "I have heard that the caribou did not come."

"What did your people do?" I asked.

"Some died."

Food now was the constant thing upon our mind. Every waking moment was fixed on the creeping weakness in our bodies, the growling, knife-sharp hunger in our guts. Thanadelthur showed me bushes – I knew their tiny flowers in the summer – that had dried red berries. We gathered some, kept some in bags, held some in our mouths until they thawed, then chewed them as we walked. They had a pleasant, slightly bitter taste. The temperature was now dropping fast. We stopped at a frozen pond where the fish were safely under six feet of ice. We broke off cattail stems and tied them into a bundle with clumsy freezing hands while two ravens croaked at us from the trees. That night we shovelled with our snowshoes, looked for scraps of firewood. While I made a tiny fire, Thanadelthur chopped the berries, reeds and leaves and made a thin, starvation soup.

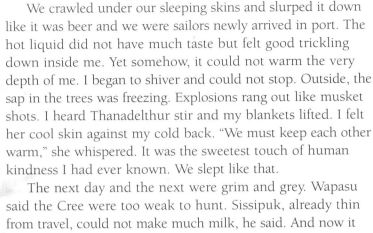

We crawled under our sleeping skins and slurped it down like it was beer and we were sailors newly arrived in port. The hot liquid did not have much taste but felt good trickling down inside me. Yet somehow, it could not warm the very depth of me. I began to shiver and could not stop. Outside, the sap in the trees was freezing. Explosions rang out like musket shots. I heard Thanadelthur stir and my blankets lifted. I felt her cool skin against my cold back. "We must keep each other warm," she whispered. It was the sweetest touch of human kindness I had ever known. We slept like that.

The next day and the next were grim and grey. Wapasu said the Cree were too weak to hunt. Sissipuk, already thin from travel, could not make much milk, he said. And now it came with blood. Thanadelthur and I shuffled out to search for firewood and found a dead tree standing. But we were too weak to push it over or even chop it down. We snapped off small branches and, exhausted, stumbled back.

As the fire caught, we lay there warming our hands when we heard the dogs yelping. Then nothing. A few minutes later, there was a sound of snowshoes at our tent. A cough. Someone threw something down then walked away. Thanadelthur peeked out the flap. A hind leg lay in the snow. Someone had killed some dogs.

Thanadelthur grabbed it, skinned it; threw it in the pot. We watched hungrily with sunken eyes and before it was done, she pulled it out. We took turns tearing at the meat. When we finished, we sucked all the marrow from the bone, then spooned the cooking pot dry.

Fuelled by the stringy carcass, we rose again. Thanadelthur set some snares for the snow-white hare and ptarmigan. I scavenged for wood, but there was never enough. The wind was up again, blowing from the north. We melted more snow, then crawled under the blankets to wait for it to boil. Tired and weak, we faded in and out of sleep. Suddenly Thanadelthur stirred. Pulling away from me, reached for her knife and began cutting one of our caribou skin bags, the one we used to carry food.

"What are you doing?"

"We must eat or die and I refuse to die without seeing my people," she said, briskly slicing the bag into small strips. She threw them into the pot. "When these are gone, we will eat our blankets, then we'll eat our clothes," she said. "We will not die." We ate in silence, perhaps because it took all our effort to chew this grisly fare.

A great wail awoke us in the morning. A long, human cry. I looked out to see several Cree gathered by Wapasu's tent. "What is it?" I asked, pulling on my mittens.

"The baby has gone to the spirit world."

Perhaps I was too numb to feel much, even grief, or perhaps I just felt that it was inevitable, given our bleak circumstance. Still, I was honour-bound to offer my condolences, and so, for the first time, Thanadelthur and I entered a Cree tent. It was dark, crowded with men and women sitting in a circle. I looked at Wapasu, but could not catch his eye as he stared without seeing. Beside him, Sissipuk sat moaning, rocking a bundle of fur clutched to her breast. Some of the women chanted softly, some wept.

After a long while, Wapasu said something. Sissipuk put the bundle down, opened it. The naked bairn was grey-blue, scrawny as a rabbit, with its tiny fist fixed to its hungry mouth. After more prayers were said, two women rewrapped the child tightly and with Sissipuk and Wapasu in the lead, we went outside. We trudged through the snowdrifts to the closest, tallest tree. Tenderly, Wapasu took his daughter from the women, held her up to the cruel grey sky and offered his child to the care of the Great Spirit. He placed the bundle in a crook of a branch, as high as he could reach and tied her there. Then he sprinkled tobacco around the tree. It was done.

I thought then of old James Knight. His grand strategy had claimed its first innocent victim.

The next morning, we awoke to sounds in camp. It was still dark when Thanadelthur looked out. "Many Cree are leaving."

I shot up like a grouse, dressed, and rushed out. It was true. Thirty, maybe more, had already taken down their tents and packed their sleds. I could not blame them, did not even think to stop them.

"Wait!" I called to a group talking with Wapasu. "I want you to take something back."

I rushed into the tent and tore a sheet from my journal, which I had all but given up. With a blackened stick from the fire, I wrote a rough note to Mr. Knight, my hands shaking wildly.

"We are in a starving condition. We have eaten nothing these eight days, I do not think I shall see you again, but I have a good heart."

Yuletide
the Christmas season

garrulous
talkative or wordy

This message I wrapped tightly in a small skin, knotted it with a cord and rushed back out. "Here, please take this to Mr. Knight at York Fort," I said, thrusting it into the hands of one of the hunters. "He will reward you generously for your trouble."

In truth, I had little hope that this dire missive would ever reach its intended destination. We watched them leave, a tattered and forlorn company and all hope I had for this enterprise went with them. The void they left behind filled me with despair.

Once again, no animals offered themselves to Thanadelthur's snares, or to our remaining hunters. Our shrunken party staggered on. "The caribou will come," the people said. That night, Thanadelthur's knife found food once again inside our tent. "See," she said brightly as she cut up one of our skins and threw the pieces in the pot. "There is game right under our nose."

"If we use up our blankets, we will freeze at night."

"Then I will have to warm you." My spirits raised a little at the mischief in her eye.

I reached over to my journal, flipped to the empty pages, ripped some out and tore them into bite-sized bits. She said nothing as I stirred them into the thin broth. But later, as we ate our desperate gruel, Thanadelthur smiled. "This is almost good. We may have to eat your map to the yellow metal."

"At this point, I do not care. I would trade it all for a juicy roast."

That night, as our thin bodies huddled, shivering together, we both dreamed of food. I saw the mess table at the fort, groaning with a Yuletide feast, Mr. Knight red-faced at the head of it, before a garrulous company. The pewter mugs sloshed over with beer. There were glistening roasts of venison, goose and duck, with low mountains of steaming potatoes and cabbage. There was raisin pudding and brandy for dessert. We drank heartily, laughed and sang and gorged ourselves, wiping the bloody juice from our chins with our sleeves.

Wake up!

"Wake up!" Thanadelthur was shaking me. I could tell by the light in the tent that we had slept late. It did not matter. We were all too weak to travel far. "I had a dream," she said, "of caribou." She rose and slipped into her clothes. "Hurry!"

"Why should I hurry? Because of your dream?" I clung hungrily to the tattered remnants of mine. I could swear that the smell of roast was in my nose. I tried to lick my lips, but my tongue was thick for want of spittle. My lips were split, as parched as driftwood.

"You must come!" There was an urgency in Thanadelthur's voice. I knew enough to obey. "I saw a caribou in my dream. A lone caribou behind a big boulder. Hurry. Bring your long gun."

I rushed from the tent. Thanadelthur was tying on her snowshoes, her breath steaming like a carriage horse, impatient to be leaving. Our camp was deathly quiet. The Cree were in no hurry either. The eastern sky was blood red as our snowshoes shuffled through thick powder. I had not fired my gun, though I kept it ready enough. The Cree did all the hunting; they preferred to. And since we'd left their land, they seldom used their guns, preferring silent deadly arrows instead, fearful lest a shot give our location away.

Thanadelthur raced ahead through the thin trees, her weakness forgotten. I marvelled at how a dream could fuel her feet. My own head ached, my body ached. Only my musket was ready, loaded with powder and lead ball. She stopped in front of me, crouched down. In a clearing just ahead, a huge rock was piled high with snow, the top blown clear. She pulled off a mitten, wet a finger in her mouth and stuck it in the air. "Go that way," she whispered, motioning to the downwind side. I crouched, my aches forgotten, my heart racing with the hunt. I crept up behind the rock, cocked the gun, readied the tinder box with the glowing ember I'd retrieved from our fire. I peeked around. A caribou cow! Not thirty feet away, it pawed at the snow. I could hear the lichen tearing as she pulled it, hear the crunching as she chewed. Then she turned and looked my way. I retreated, blew on the glowing ember, touched the fuse, stepped out and raised my gun. It shook in my weakened arms. My hot breath rose in front of me, blinding me. Then the gun went off.

The roar echoed in the clearing. Half-blinded now by smoke, I saw the cow leap into the air and whirl around, searching for the thing that bit her. On her rear right flank a bright red hole was trickling blood. She snorted, whirled again, painting the snow with drops of red as she let out a long,

tinder box
a metal box for carrying material used to make a fire, or in this case, a glowing ember from the fire

painful cry. Down dropped her hind quarters, but still her front legs pawed as she struggled to get up.

Something raced past me like a wolf. Thanadelthur! She ran up behind the thrashing cow. Throwing herself across its back, she drove her knife down into it. There was another horrendous cry, I don't know whose. The knife raised, then plunged again. Suddenly, all was quiet. I watched Thanadelthur raise her head. She was giving thanks.

There was a soft sound behind me. It was Wapasu and a handful of Cree, armed for fighting with guns and spears. They lowered them when they saw us. "You are a hunter," Wapasu said, with praise in his voice. We moved to the kill where Thanadelthur knelt in the snow. She raised her head; her mouth was covered in blood. She'd been drinking from a wound. She rose, wiped her red mouth with her mitten and grinned a bloody grin.

"You see," she said to me. "We must listen to our dreams."

The Cree hunters offered their own quick prayers and a sprinkling of tobacco, then sent for the women. Sissipuk and four others came quickly. Even her sad eyes brightened at the sight. "Where are the others?" I asked, counting only ten Cree in the clearing.

"The others have gone," said Wapasu.

"When?"

"Yesterday. They went ahead to search for game." He paused, then added, "It is better this way. Maybe they sent this caribou."

We fell on the animal like a pack of hungry wolves. Carving off red chunks of flesh still steaming warm, we threw them in our mouths. In minutes, the caribou was butchered, its skin and meat bundled onto a sleigh. The women pulled it back to camp as the four remaining dogs chewed happily on bones and gristle.

We feasted, and strengthened by this nourishment, chopped down a few dead standing trees and built a bonnie fire. Over it swung the juicy drizzling roasts of my dreams. Perhaps because of our timely kill, perhaps because our numbers were so reduced, we laughed and talked together as never before. Our shrunken stomachs revolted at the sudden quantities of food. We ran off from the fire, retched it up and came back laughing, ready for more. The women built a rack and smoked some of surplus meat for the hunters. The rest would keep well frozen. They scraped the hide clean. The bones went into bubbling pots of soup. That night, as we sat around the outside fire together, the Cree and Thanadelthur told stories of their people: tales of great hunters and feats of courage. And later, as we lay beneath our sleeping skins, drowsy, full and warm,

94

a wolf howled. In the silence we held our breath, waiting for an answering call and smiling when it came. "Life is good," I thought. "Very, very good."

T he next day, our diminished party moved on. There were but twelve of us now, ten Cree, Thanadelthur and me. But even though the days were often grey with blowing, drifting snow, our spirits were much restored and we chatted as we trudged along. We crossed three more frozen rivers and two vast white lakes. As we moved northward, the trees grew smaller and sometimes, the land opened up into great white moving vistas of snow. "I know we are close," Thanadelthur told me.

"Stop!" said Wapasu suddenly, late one afternoon. He looked around and checked the wind. "I smell smoke," he said.

My heart quickened at the thought and I looked at Thanadelthur. Her eyes danced, but our Cree were cautious as we approached their old enemies. Wapasu motioned to Thanadelthur.

"You lead," he said. "They will recognize your pointy coat." As she moved to the front, Wapasu waved our four warriors into the woods. They would travel there beside us, to surprise the enemy if we were attacked. Thanadelthur launched herself forward, with Wapasu behind her, then me and the four women with our packs and the one remaining dog sled.

"Hello," yelled Thanadelthur as she strode along, her snowshoes kicking up a flurry of powdery snow. "I am Dene. I have come home to the land where the spirit flows."

We rounded some rocks and a small clump of bush. Thanadelthur stopped. Two skin tents sat ahead in the snow. A small column of smoke rose from a dying fire. And beside it – bodies.

Eeeee! "Eeeeee!" The scream was Thanadelthur's. She ran forward. "No. No. No!"

We raced behind her to the camp. The bodies lay scattered in the bloody snow. Thanadelthur ran to each of them, shrieking as she turned them, shook them. It was a grisly sight; nine people, all in pointy coats. They'd been shot, their throats all cut ... and worse.

Thanadelthur whirled on Wapasu. "You murdering snakes," she screamed, hammering him with her fists. "Your bloody Cree have killed my people." He grabbed her wrists and threw her to the snow.

His jaw clenched tightly as he inspected the bodies. The four Cree warriors, weapons ready, came warily from the trees. "The attackers have gone," one said. "South."

Weeping with deep, wrenching sobs, Thanadelthur crawled to the bodies and turned an old man face up. "This was an elder," she screamed. "He had more wisdom in his smallest toe than the pack of you Cree dogs!" Wapasu and the Cree stood still as stones. "And this," Thanadelthur turned another body, "this was someone I played with as a child." To each body she went, a whole family of her Dene people, wiped out.

Then Thanadelthur stood and faced the solemn, troubled Cree. "Only the Cree have guns. The people who travelled with us did this." She walked around, searching at the ground. "See, those are snowshoe tracks of cowardly Cree. They are not Dene, not the northern Inuit either."

Wapasu could not argue. Finally, he spoke. "Then it is finished. Tomorrow or the next day or the next day after that, we will meet your people and they will kill us to settle this score." He turned to me. "This plan of yours is dead. It died with these people. We must leave! Now! Are you coming?"

The three of us stood there, a triumvirate of grief, lost hope and sorrow. "I-I-I ..." I could not think. I broke away, struggled over to a bush and retched.

Thanadelthur stood face to face with Wapasu. Her tear-filled eyes looked up into his sad weary ones. "If you leave," she sobbed, "there will be no peace, only more killing." She straightened, making herself taller. "You have been our strong captain. You did not kill my people. Neither did your good wife, who has lost a child on this walk. Nor did these others, who have endured so much." She wiped her eyes with her mittens and sniffed. I want nothing more for my people than peace. I want them to have the things that make your lives easier; that make you better hunters, and make things better for your women. I want this for the Dene."

As she spoke, Thanadelthur seemed to grow stronger, willing Wapasu with every word. "Stay here. Stay for a week, no, ten days, while I find my people. I will tell them you did not kill this family. I will tell them you are here in peace. That you have gifts for them. And promises of more."

Wapasu's dark face frowned as he considered Thanadelthur's words. He looked around, at the fearful expressions of his warriors, at the weary faces of the women, at Sissipuk whom he loved.

"We will stay," he said. "Not here, for the spirits of these Dene people are angry and will not rest, but close by." He motioned with his hand. "We will make camp for ten days, and then we will go south."

triumvirate
a group of three; from the Latin *triumvir*, one of three men who jointly shared civic authority in ancient Rome

Thanadelthur nodded.

"I will go with you," I said.

"No. I must go alone." She gathered up a bag of smoked caribou, her knife, some snares, and a sleeping skin, which she threw across her shoulders. Then she left. As she walked away, northward through the bush, I felt a cord inside me tearing with worry and grief.

We left the Dene camp and followed Thanadelthur's tracks without speaking until we came to a large clearing. "We will camp here," Wapasu said. It was the first time we had stayed in such an open and exposed place, but I knew the Cree were fearful of a surprise attack. We pitched our tents and Wapasu posted a guard. That night, I made a small fire in our empty tent and by the flickering light, tried to write in my long-neglected journal. The words would not come. Instead, I saw frozen faces in the snow; the last one was Thanadelthur's. I shook my head to chase the hideous thought away, then fell into a troubled, fitful sleep.

The next morning, the Cree were restless and more fearful. "We are going to make a fort," said Wapasu, "to protect us from the angry Dene. I started to say something against it, but realized it was no use and soon the woods echoed with the sound of axes. There was nothing to do but help. The Cree worked quickly, removing the branches of the spruce where they fell. I dragged each pole into the clearing. The women had found some young willow nearby. They laid the poles together in a row, lashed them together with the willow along the top and bottom. We worked at this all morning and after the sun set in the afternoon, we raised the sections one by one, braced other poles against them, and made a rough circular palisade around our three remaining tents. Then the women gathered the branches we'd cut and wove them into the poles until its looked like a wild, bristling hedge of a fort. From outside, you could not see into the palisade, but from inside we could see out.

The Cree spirits improved with this fortification and the next day we went hunting. "Come join us," Wapasu said and I eagerly accepted. Only three of us went out, the rest stayed back to guard the camp. But we didn't need to go very far. Soon we came across a small herd of caribou, moving toward us across a narrow river with steep banks, deep in snow. The caribou sank up to their bellies as they struggled up the slope while we waited at the top. As they came near, their breath blowing great clouds of steam, we jumped up and fired. The terrified animals scattered, charging off in every direction, but three lay dead in the snow.

"Wait ten days, and I will return with my people."

All day we travelled back and forth, aided by the dogs and women, carrying the meat, hides and horns back to camp. After almost starving for so much of our journey, we now had more than we could eat. We dragged it inside the palisades through the little gate, and enjoyed another roast. But this time there was no feast, no celebration. Nine dead Dene lay in the snow not far away, their spirits waiting to be avenged. And somewhere, out there alone, was Thanadelthur.

That night the wind picked up. I lay alone in my tent, within earshot of the conversations of the Cree and later, of their snoring. The dogs snarled, began to bark. I looked out; there was moonlight above, and along the ground, a flurry of drifting snow. I grew fearful for Thanadelthur. What if wolves find her? What if the murdering Cree went north instead of south? I prayed to God to help her, then prayed to the Great Spirit, too. At last, feeling somewhat better, I drifted off to sleep.

There were wolf tracks in the drifts outside our fort next morning, so we built a platform in the open for the meat. We cut down four of the tallest trees we could find, built a floor of logs, then hoisted the whole thing up with cross-braces to support it, and lashed it all together with caribou cords. We made a rough ladder, too, carried the frozen meat up, and covered it with fresh hides.

Then we waited.

That was the hardest task of all. I cleaned my gun and greased it, sharpened my knife and axe. The Cree men did the same, strengthened the last dog sled, made new sleds for the women to pull. The women sewed new moccasins and mitts, mended coats, smoked caribou meat for the journey home. Three days went by, then four, then five.

I tried to write, but couldn't. I worked on my map, now on its fourteenth page, but the minutes seemed like hours and I found myself staring at the tent, seeing nothing.

"If her people are more than five days away, then she will not get back here in time," Wapasu said one night. I knew the Cree were tense. I heard them arguing at night. Some wanted to go, Wapasu had said they'd stay. If they went what would I do? Stay and wait? Go with them? What if Thanadelthur returned to an empty camp? The questions were heartbreaking, the answers even worse.

Time froze like ice. I took to walking in circles around the clearing, wearing a deep path through the snow. "You are like a wounded goose that can't take off," Sissipuk said one day. I was happy to see her smile.

"Would you show me how to make a snare?" I asked Wapasu in desperation on the eighth day. He laughed.

"Yes, it would be good for you to learn. You might end up living here." I did not understand what he meant. We looked for rabbit tracks, or where a ptarmigan might nest. With a thin cord made from hide, he showed me how to loop it from a bent branch, how to set and hide it in the snow, how to rig a stick to trip it when an animal or bird disturbed it. I set six.

The next morning we went back to check them, but I couldn't find them. Not one. Wapasu roared with laughter. My face flushed hot as I searched, Wapasu's laugh ringing in my ears. "Maybe the Trickster has tripped your snares," he said, tears in his eyes. That night around the campfire, he told the others and for the first time in a long while we all laughed. "The first rule of hunting," Wapasu said, pointing to his head, "is to remember. Remember everything." And I remembered Thanadelthur and that tomorrow was the tenth day and that we would leave.

Then the awful morning came. The Cree were anxious to go. Wapasu looked at me and shook his head. She is not coming, his eyes said. I was sick with grief. The women cooked a big soup and we ate together silently, dipping our bowls into the thick broth. I ate little and threw the rest to the dogs who lapped it up in the snow. Two of the men began taking the frozen meat off the platform and packing it on a sled. They covered it with a caribou robe, tied it down with thongs. One of the women pulled down a tent.

And then we heard it. A cry, a croaking rasping cry, like a raven. The men who'd been outside the palisade rushed in and shut the gate. "That woman is back!" they said.

I pushed past them, tore open the gate and rushed out. There, at the edge of the clearing stood Thanadelthur, smiling – the loveliest sight in all Creation. Behind her, in the trees, stood twenty, no fifty, perhaps a hundred Dene in their pointed coats.

When she saw me, Thanadelthur began to run. I broke into a run to meet her. Vaguely I heard Wapasu call my name. I ignored him, running without snowshoes along the path through the snow. We hugged. I grabbed

Trickster
in many native American cultures, a mythological creature with the ability to transform himself into many shapes, to play tricks on humans and teach them lessons. Some cultures believed the Trickster was a coyote.

her, lifting her up. "Thanadelthur." It was all I could say. She laughed, her dark eyes dancing. Then she remembered her people and pushed my arms away.

Blushing, she turned to look at them waiting in the trees. "There are proper ways to do this," she said to me, her voice almost gone. "They have never seen one of you before, and they are very frightened by the Cree."

"Well, lass," I pointed toward the bristling fort. "I don't know who's more frightened but now at least, it's not me." I touched her again to make sure that she was real. "What happened to your voice?"

"Too much talking," she said. "I will tell you later."

"Wapasu!" she called. "Come out. Put down your long muskets and your spears. Bring only your pipes and tobacco. And the gifts. I have brought a hundred of my who people wish to trade and live in peace."

We waited. Nothing moved. One hundred pairs of wary eyes at the edge of the clearing, ten pairs of frightened eyes inside the palisades. Finally, the gate opened. Wapasu walked out, followed by the five warriors and behind them, the women. Their eyes squinted as they looked for their ancient enemies in the shadows of the forest.

"Call out your people," Wapasu said. "We cannot see them all."

Thanadelthur turned to the forest. "Come," she croaked. "Do not be afraid. They have put down their long guns. They are outnumbered and wish to talk." Slowly, some of the Dene warriors began to move toward the place where Thanadelthur and I stood. "Throw down your weapons, Dene people," she rasped. "Do you want to live like hunted rabbits? Do you want the constant threat of war?"

But only a few came out. "We are afraid," said one man. "We are afraid of the Cree guns that kill us with a puff of smoke."

Thanadelthur stamped her feet in disgust. Whirling around, she ran back, grabbed some women by their coats and pulled them out of the trees into the clearing. "Do you want war or peace?" she pleaded. "Do you want sharp knives and guns that mean your children will never go hungry again?" She ran to an older man. "Uncle, show some courage or these Cree will laugh at the Dene children hiding."

Slowly, a few more of the Dene began to move into the clearing. Thanadelthur took heart. "See," she said. "Years from now around our fires, whose names will be remembered from this day? Not those names of cowards who cling to the trees. Only the brave will be known in our stories."

She ran back toward me, then stopped as a few more Dene emerged from the trees and slowly followed. "Yes, yes, come with me. Let us smoke the peace pipe. Let me show you the wonderful gifts we have brought."

The Dene could not withstand the barrage issuing from this fiery, croaking marten. In twos and threes, they straggled forward and stood silently behind her in the snow.

Only when the last Dene had come did Thanadelthur turn again and smile. "Wapasu, my people are ready to talk with your people now."

Behind me the Cree had stopped, just as scared, just as wary. Thanadelthur pointed to a tall Dene warrior behind her. "This is my brother, Thekulthili. He will speak for my people." Her eyes were fierce with pride.

As is the custom in this country, we sat down in the snow. In my halting Dene words, I retold the story of our journey, of Mr. Knight and his desire to trade Dene furs for English things of value. Wapasu spoke next, and Thanadelthur translated as the Cree captain repeated the purpose of the mission and told the story of the trip. Behind us sat the Cree and Dene, listening to every word as the faint sun travelled slowly across the sky.

Thanadelthur's voice was little more than a whisper now. After the stories had been told, she nodded to Wapasu and asked him to light the peace pipe. The four of us moved closer. As we sat and smoked, Sissipuk brought my pack full of gifts from James Knight.

Thanadelthur rose and handed gifts to all her people, making sure that no one was left out. The shadows grew long and new fires were lit outside the palisade. The caribou meat was unpacked and slowly the people began to crowd together, making signs, because no words were the same in their languages. A great feast was held. And the sound of Dene and Cree drums rang throughout the cold forest under the watchful Wolf Star.

It was decided that ten Dene would return with us, including Thekulthili. We would bring them to York Fort where Mr. Knight would give them even more gifts. We left the next morning.

One day during our travels, Thanadelthur told Thekulthili of my map and he asked to see it. I showed him the pictures of all the rivers and lakes we'd seen and where we'd met in the clearing. He took my quill, made a long mark nearby, then another, to the north and east. "These are the rivers that have the yellow metal," he said.

barrage
a concentrated out-pouring of something – words, blows or weapon fire

The return trip took more than 100 days but the late winter was kinder, the caribou were plentiful, and we did not starve again. We heard the snow geese flying north again and on May 6th, 1716, we came to the Nelson River. It was a warm night and the earth was fragrant with spring. The next morning, a flotilla of Home Cree paddled by. Wapasu called to them, but when they saw the strange Dene, they were frightened. We assured them they were safe and I gave my musket to one of them in return for ferrying us across. As I stepped ashore, a Cree paddler threw my carrying bag to me. It was a careless toss and I missed it. The bag splashed into the water and sank.

Royal Jack
another name for the British flag

Thanadelthur's eyes grew large in horror. "Your journal! Your maps!"

I laughed. "I don't care a whit. We're so close to home I can taste it."

Together we walked along the eight-mile path we'd walked almost a year before. When we came to the Hayes, we turned east and soon we saw the Royal Jack flying on the pole. They were the brightest colours I'd seen in a year – except for snow and sky and blood – and I remembered that there were things in the world such as pewter mugs of beer, dishes piled high with stove-cooked food, and deep mattresses of down. Then the Home Cree came running, children and dogs in the lead. Behind them were Company servants and soldiers, and then James Knight, looking as haggard as if he had made the trip himself.

He clapped me on the back, pumped my hand, then gave Thanadelthur a crushing hug. "I'd given you up for dead," he said, "after I got that awful note."

"We might well have been," I said as we walked toward the fort. "Wapasu was a brave and able leader, but it was Thanadelthur who was the chief instrument of our success." I looked around. Wapasu was well behind us, Thanadelthur was dragging her brother ahead. "Sir, she has a devilish spirit and I believe that if there were fifty more Dene like her, they'd drive the Cree clear out of the country." Mr. Knight laughed a hearty laugh. "Aye, thanks to her, now you can build that new trading post of yours up on the Churchill River."

And there it is, my friend, as long and cold a tale as any I've told. I must beg your kind forgiveness if I've kept you, for I see the fire is gone and there's naught but glowing embers in this rocky pit.

There is, I hasten to add, a postscript. But do not worry; I will make quick work of it if you will bear with me. Upon her successful and heroic return, Thanadelthur took a husband, one of the Dene who came back with us. Yet, because the Company ship was late that year and there were no supplies with which to build the promised Churchill fort, Mr. Knight wanted to send her out again to let her people know. And she gladly would have gone, would have left her man behind if need be, so strongly did she want to bring English goods to her people.

But the Great Spirit had other plans for her. That January, shortly after Yuletide, a sickness swept through the draughty fort. And when it brought Thanadelthur down, no one thought it strange. But while others recovered, she did not. Instead, she went from bad to worse. Old Mr. Knight was, to say the least, distraught. He stayed by her side morning and night, raging at the surgeon to heal her, gentle as a nurse as he wiped the fever from her brow. She seemed not to care for her health, but she was so determined that her people get new goods that she taught a young English lad her Dene tongue, in her last feverish days. Then she died. She was buried at the fort on February 5th, 1717.

It was the fairest day we'd seen all winter, as Mr. Knight remarked, and surely the most melancholy of his life.

I do suspect her death unhinged us both. I travelled south toward Albany Fort after our return, endured another awful winter, and the following summer went to Churchill, for our Company ship had finally come. But my heart was no longer in this enterprise. I had frightful dreams, of starving on the barren land, or freezing in my tent. And I awoke several times to find that they'd locked me in a cupboard or tied me to my soaking bed. I'd eaten my belt, they said, and was about to eat my boots. And during one of these lunatic spells, I died.

Ach, I do apologize if that takes you by surprise. I would have thought you'd noticed my gaunt appearance. I hasten to tell you then that Mr. Knight himself would soon be in the same boat, as the English sailors like to say. With mourning black still wrapped around his heart, he sailed back to England and appealed to the stern and august men of the Hudson's Bay Committee to give him two ships. To find the Northwest Passage, he told them, because Thanadelthur had said there was a salty sea with tides to the north of where her people lived. They gave him a frigate and a sloop. And they also agreed to give him a goodly portion of all the gold and copper

aurora
high altitude, many coloured lights that flash across the northern skies at night. They are thought to be caused by charged solar particles that are captured by Earth's magnetic field. Also called aurora borealis or northern lights (or over Australia, aurora australis or southern lights).

lunatic
insane, suffering from mental illness. The original meaning of the word had to do with the belief that some forms of mental illness were associated with the phases of the moon (luna).

she'd told him he would find. It was only the gleam that kept him going. But back here in the bay, as his two ships poked into coves and inlets, searching for the icy shortcut to Cathay, they were overtaken by a storm and run hard aground here on Marble Island. And this is where they waited, and tended this pitiful fire, watching for a ship that never came. One by one they slowly starved and froze to death, leaving the polar bears and wolves to argue over their glistening bones.

I see that you're rising now and about to leave this grisly place. I can't say I blame you, for we, too, are going. Look! There is Thanadelthur now, radiant in her pointy caribou gown, and Mr. James Knight, looking his more youthful self, and I, my ruddy health restored. And we three souls are going for a walk together upon the land. The next time you are out and away from your civilized places, and you hear the loon's forlorn call, the whisper of the wind, or the honking of geese in some darkened sky below the shimmering aurora, it may be us passing by. We will be heading north.

Cathay
an older word for China

Mike Macri

The cairn at Churchill honouring Thanadelthur overlooks the northern landscape she loved.

In 2001, the Historic Sites and Monuments Board of Canada designated Thanadelthur as a National Historic Person. Her nomination for this recognition came from the Churchill Ladies Club of Churchill, Manitoba, and was supported by Chief Galdys Powderhorn and the Sayisi Dene First Nation of Tadoule Lake, Manitoba. The Churchill Ladies Club had also erected a plaque to honour Thanadelthur in 1967, and there is a street in the community named after her.

Bibliography

Blackships

The Voyages of Jacques Cartier, by Jacques Cartier, translated by H.P. Biggar (1924), with an introduction by Ramsay Cook, University of Toronto Press, 1993

The Face of Paris, Harold P. Clunn, Spring Books, London, 1958

Beneath The Cross: Catholics and Huguenots in Sixteenth-Century Paris, Barbara B. Diefendorf, Oxford University Press, 1991

Canada: A People's History, Don Gilmor & Pierre Turgeon, Canadian Broadcasting Corporation, McClelland & Stewart, 2000

Exploring the Fur Trade Routes of North America: A Time Traveller's Guide, Barbara Huck, Heartland Associates Inc., 2000

Canada Rediscovered, Robert McGhee, Canadian Museum of Civilization, 1991

Saint-Malo Historique, Édouard Prampain, Amiens, Piteux Frères, Éditeurs, 1902

People of the Longhouse: How The Iroquoian Tribes Lived, by Jillian & Robin Ridington, Douglas & McIntyre, 1982

The Children of Aataentsic: A History of the Huron People to 1660, Dr. Bruce G. Trigger, McGill-Queen's University Press, 1987

Natives and Newcomers: Canada's "Heroic Age" Reconsidered, Dr. Bruce G. Trigger, McGill-Queen's University Press, 1985

Saint-Malo Histoire Générale, Deuxième Édition revue et audmentée, François Tuloup, Ouvrage couronné par l'académie française

Six Chapters of Canada's Pre-History, by J.V. Wright, National Museum of Man, Ottawa 1976

Thanadelthur

Daily Life on Western Hudson's Bay 1714-1870: A Social History of York Factory and Churchill, by Michael Payne, doctoral dissertation, Carleton University, Ottawa, 1988.

Drum Songs: Glimpses of Dene History, by Kerry Abel, McGill-Queen's University Press, 1993

Inkonze: The Stones of Traditional Knowledge, by Phillip R. Coutu and Lorraine Hoffman-Mercredi, Thunderwoman Ethnographics, 1999

Letters From Hudson Bay 1701–40, K.G. Davies (General Editor), The Hudson's Bay Record Society, Volume XXV, London, 1965

"Love of Life," a short story from *The Call of the Wild*, by Jack London, Penguin Classics, 1986

Many Tender Ties: Women in Fur-Trade Society in Western Canada, 1670–1870, by Sylvia Van Kirk, Watson & Dwyer Publishing Ltd., 1986

Running West, by James Houston, McClelland & Stewart Inc., 1989

Strangers Devour the Land, by Boyce Richardson, The Macmillan Company of Canada Limited, 1975

Strangers in Blood: Fur Trade Company Families in Indian Country, by Jennifer H.S. Brown, The University of British Columbia Press, 1980.

The Most Respected Place in the Territory: Everyday Life in Hudson's Bay Company Service York Factory, 1788–1870, by Michael Payne, Canadian Parks Service, 1989

The Canadian Indian: The Illustrated History of the Great Tribes of Canada, Fraser Symington, McClelland & Stewart Limited, 1969

"Thanadelthur", by Sylvia Van Kirk, an article in *The Beaver*, Spring, 1974

Walking on the Land, by Farley Mowat, Key Porter Books, Toronto, 2000

Wild Coffee and Tea Substitutes of Canada, Nancy J. Turner and Adam F. Szezawinski, National Museum of Natural Sciences, 1978